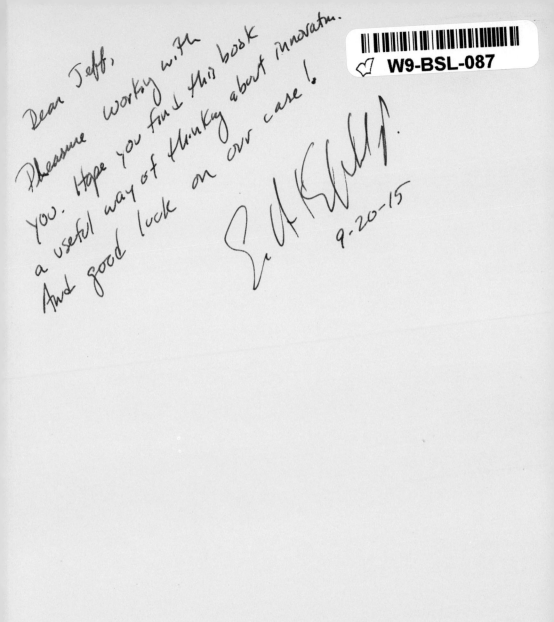

Dear Jeff,

Pleasure working with you. Hope you find this book a useful way of thinking about innovation. And good luck on our case!

9-20-15

INSIDE REAL
INNOVATION

**How the Right Approach Can Move Ideas from
R&D to Market — And Get the Economy Moving**

INSIDE REAL INNOVATION

How the Right Approach Can Move Ideas from R&D to Market — And Get the Economy Moving

Eugene Fitzgerald & Andreas Wankerl

Massachusetts Institute of Technology, School of Engineering
Cornell University, Johnson School of Management
The Innovation Interface

Carl Schramm

The Kauffman Foundation

 World Scientific

NEW JERSEY · LONDON · SINGAPORE · BEIJING · SHANGHAI · HONG KONG · TAIPEI · CHENNAI

Published by

World Scientific Publishing Co. Pte. Ltd.

5 Toh Tuck Link, Singapore 596224

USA office: 27 Warren Street, Suite 401-402, Hackensack, NJ 07601

UK office: 57 Shelton Street, Covent Garden, London WC2H 9HE

British Library Cataloguing-in-Publication Data
A catalogue record for this book is available from the British Library.

First published 2011
Reprinted 2012, 2013

INSIDE REAL INNOVATION
How the Right Approach Can Move Ideas from R&D to Market — And Get
the Economy Moving

ISBN-13 978-981-4327-98-5
ISBN-10 981-4327-98-0

Printed in Singapore by B & Jo Enterprise Pte Ltd

To Michelle, Danielle and Patrick

Preface

This book is a departure on two fronts. It describes the details of the innovation process at the practical level, using a new model to explain how the process really occurs. Then it connects this to macro-level implications for a nation's economy, addressing the various stakeholders in innovation. Most books about innovation have been based on high-level observations, but if one does not take into account how the process unfolds at the practical or micro-level, conclusions can be erroneous. At the heart of the matter is the fact that innovation is a process performed by *people*, not by organizations.

But even the best innovators cannot operate in a vacuum. They work in an environment of multiple institutions, such as corporations, investment firms, universities, and government agencies, each providing the settings or support for particular activities in particular ways. These institutions — and how they operate, and how they interrelate — determine the nature of the country's innovation "pipeline" or "system." Innovators have to think and plan and interact within this system, and their innovations have to travel through it in order to arrive, eventually, in usable form at a marketplace.

Many policy measures are aimed at tweaking and adjusting the system to enhance the output. Meanwhile, various actors and entities within the system also are making changes, whether to achieve the same end or to improve their own outcomes, often both. Naturally, everyone involved needs a good understanding of what results their actions might have. This is especially true at a time when the system is in crisis, when it has evolved to a tenuous transition stage where it is no longer fit to support and deliver innovation as it once did, and has not reached a new and fitter form, either.

We, the authors, contend that such a crisis is under way in the United States. Our hope is that this book will contribute to a better understanding of how to proceed. Readers in the U.S. have an obvious stake in the matter, and the book is written from a U.S. perspective, but what's presented here can be useful to readers in any country.

We write from the basis of extensive practical experience in innovation and the commercialization of new technology. We have worked across multiple institutions through decades of system evolution. Without boasting, we think we can say this makes us especially able to drill down into the details of the innovation process and connect them to the larger picture. Some readers may wish to skim the details of the process, gleaning what they need in order to understand the implications at the macro-level. However, we encourage everyone to study all chapters, as the details are important to anyone wanting to take fruitful action.

Acknowledgments

A number of people who influenced and inspired us are mentioned in the course of this book. Much of what is written here about the links between research and practical innovation stems from co-author Gene Fitzgerald's experiences at AT&T Bell Laboratories from 1988-1994; Gene thanks all his former colleagues there for the opportunity to work in one of history's great innovation factories.

Gene and Andreas Wankerl began formally developing the concepts of the book around 2006, when Andreas launched the Business of Science and Technology Initiative at Cornell University. This program piloted new ideas about corporate-university interfaces for both the learning and advancement of innovation, and we thank all who were visionary in supporting it, including the Johnson Graduate School of Management and the College of Engineering at Cornell. Key individuals were Richard Schafer, Robert Swieringa, Kent Fuchs, Joseph Thomas, Robert Buhrman, Abby Westervelt, Emmanuel Giannelis, Randy Allen and Christopher Ober. The dedicated Cornell alumni who seeded our ideas with initial funding were John and Elaine Alexander, John V. Balen, Jeff Berg and Debra Paget, Jason J. Hogg, and Roy H. Park, Jr.

The Ewing Marion Kauffman Foundation provided an intellectual sounding board for our emerging concepts. Gene thanks Lesa Mitchell for pulling him into this rich environment, and for introducing us to our collaborator and third co-author, Carl Schramm. The Foundation also funded the expansion of our corporate-university interface work, which eventually led us to form a nonprofit entity to house that work, The Innovation

Interface (www.innovationinterface.org). Guy DiCicco, a collaborator in The Innovation Interface, has been an invaluable partner both practically and intellectually.

The Massachusetts Institute of Technology has played key roles throughout. MIT is at the heart of an entire, vibrant ecosystem for innovation and new business activity, within which Gene has practiced and learned hands-on since leaving Bell Labs in 1994. Gene cherishes the time spent building AmberWave with Dr. Mayank Bulsara and other early participants in the company. MIT has been an ideal setting for our further experiments with the formal teaching of innovation; the school's Industrial Liaison Program has been a valued partner as well. We are thankful to our partner in teaching innovation at MIT, Dr. Arne Hessenbruch. The Singapore-MIT Alliance has expanded the teaching globally while enriching our international perspectives on innovation and growth, and World Scientific Press of Singapore has done fine work in publishing this book.

As for the writing: Mike Vargo, an independent editor in the U.S., worked with us to review and revise the first draft. We thank him for improving the book tremendously. And above all we thank everyone who is working right now, in his or her own way, to improve the human condition through innovation.

Contents

Chapter 1

The Innovation Crisis

"The money changers have fled from their high seats in the temple of our civilization. We may now restore that temple to the ancient truths."

Franklin D. Roosevelt
Inaugural Address, March 4, 1933

As the United States economy staggered through the booms and busts of the first decade of the 2000s, the hunt for scapegoats began, as it always does in troubled times. Where are the people who did this? Who fumbled away our jobs, drained our budgets and wiped out the value of our portfolios? As usual, it was easy to blame the moneychangers: the financiers and speculators, the investment gurus who proclaim what our dollars should be put into. And there have been plenty of signs pointing to the money people as the guilty parties.

The scapegoat narrative may make an interesting story, but in this book our interest is the real story. Free market economies have cycles; corrections are natural and necessary; and sometimes rules need to be adjusted as well. But when a slump has been profound and prolonged, the challenge is to look beneath the symptoms to see what is going on underneath. In this case, the financial crisis has masked a serious underlying problem that needs to be addressed. The problem has been eating away at the country's basic ability to generate and sustain economic growth. If we want to restore the economy to real vitality, instead of just settling for periodic upticks in the vital signs, we need to deal with the fact that beneath the financial crisis, we have an innovation crisis.

Innovation — the process of putting ideas into useful form and bringing them to market — is the true engine of economic growth. This has been true since ancient times, although only fully recognized in modern times. These "ideas put into useful form" have enabled us to raise our productivity, whether it's by plowing fields more efficiently with an iron-bladed plow, by restoring our health with an antibiotic — or by flying like a bird except much faster, in a machine that also can transport a wagon train's worth of goods. Some of the most powerful innovations are those for which we find so many uses that the benefits keep multiplying: computers are now so valuable in every walk of life that it can be hard to remember they were first created, literally, for computing. Fundamental innovations of this kind have the power to create multiple companies and multiple industries. The resulting *innovation paradigms* can generate economic growth for decades.

And the most powerful growth-driver of all is what makes it all happen, the human process of innovating. Despite the fact that we humans are the ones doing it, the workings of this process are still not widely understood. Only in recent times have we begun to grasp the immense value of assuring that the process runs well, and finding ways to help it run better. The crisis, as we shall see, is the manifestation of changing conditions that have disrupted the support system for innovation, allowing the process to sputter and run down — even as we were busy reaping its benefits. All sectors, not only the financial sector, have been both culprits and victims in letting this occur.

The invitation of this book is to open the hood and see what has gone wrong. All who are willing to inspect the engine and its problems, and roll up their sleeves and contribute to fixing it, will stand to gain tremendously.

Certainly financiers have played a part in the crisis, as evidenced by misguided investment during the dot-com and telecom bubbles of the late 1990s, the first of a series of bubbles. That was hardly surprising. Towards the end of long periods of sustained growth, it is not uncommon to see finance become detached from reality. Ages of great innovation create great wealth, and for some time, returns are re-invested efficiently to feed growth to even greater heights. But invariably, the abundance of wealth creates a dangerous luxury. It allows a growing percentage of financiers to operate at a level of abstraction where they lose sight of the details of how wealth is really produced.

Which is essentially what happened during the dot-com and telecom bubbles. Investors saw the Internet and other IT industries taking off; they saw new companies emerging with new ideas for those markets; and many of them simply set out to connect the dots as directly as possible: "go fast and go big, or go home". Many of the details in between, the details of what it actually takes to innovate successfully, were either overlooked or misunderstood. Expectation of high returns, coupled with incorrect assessment of cost and risk, became the dominant driving force and ultimately a recipe for disaster.

A series of other investment-driven bubbles ensued, collapsed and brought grief, along with a much-needed correction to many market values, but they did not bring the degree of clarity now needed by all of us for dealing with the deeper issues. Hazy thinking about innovation has persisted across society, even amid the growing awareness that something is awry.

A number of observers have noted that the country's "innovation pipeline" seems to be drying up. There hasn't been a sustained flow of new products and industries like those that fueled growth in the late twentieth century, they point out. The general observation is correct, but most of the cures that are proposed would be partial solutions at best, unlikely to produce anything near the economic impact expected of them.

For example many policy makers urge the nation to pump more money into scientific research, so as to fill the pipeline with new stuff that will re-invigorate the American colossus. After all, we know what has happened before, right? Researchers think deep thoughts and discover things, our competitive marketplace picks the best ideas to pull through the pipeline, and products come out the end to propel the U.S. to further economic success. So let's prime the pump!

This is considered a forward-looking line of thinking, but it connects the dots much too simply. Of course it is good to invest in basic research. Good arguments can be made for investing more. But to begin with, innovation is not a straight-line process, as most people believe it to be when picturing the invention of the light bulb straight through to patent, prototype, and product. As we'll see in the next chapter it is a highly iterative process, and the iterations do not consist merely of trying the same task again and again, as Edison did to find the right filament material for his light bulb. The iterations typically include juggling and re-considering many technical and business factors, with an ever-changing view of how you might implement the idea, and the markets that are likely to be interested. Gradually you arrive at a new "product" and a new "business" that might be quite different from what you first envisioned.

Doing this well is not easy. It has to be done within an environment, or system, which is capable of supporting all the diverse iterations, interactions and transactions needed. People have to learn or obtain what they need from the right other people, and money for the right activity has to be put in at the right time. *This whole enabling-and-support system is what constitutes the "pipeline"*. Like any pipeline, it "carries" what moves through it; it carries the innovation process.

Furthermore, it is an error of abstraction to think of the innovation pipeline as something separate from the larger macroeconomic system. It is often thought of that way, as a sort of free-standing machine: you put in your research money, the marketplace selects the product it wants, and after some clicking and whirring, out it comes. Not at all. That is the wrong metaphor entirely.

The innovation pipeline is an integral part of the macroeconomic system; think of it as embedded in that system. And now, due to a confluence of events, the earth has shifted, breaking and disjointing the pipeline in key places. The innovation *process* that it carries has begun to stall, or to seep away in wasteful directions far off the optimal path. Crumbling infrastructure, indeed.

Many of us have sensed the seismic nature of the shifts, not only in the U.S. but in other countries whose innovation pipelines are now interconnected with that of the U.S., or that emulate it in certain respects. It is small wonder then that so many are uneasy, feeling insecure about the prospects of restoring growth any time soon. As Thomas Kuhn pointed out in *The Structure of Scientific Revolutions*, a known predecessor to a paradigm shift is a pronounced and undefined anxiety by those participating in the current paradigm.

It is not uncommon to project this anxiety onto external factors, such as the economic reforms in parts of China and in India that have seemed to further threaten America's leadership across the innovation spectrum. Both countries, along with others in Asia, began achieving what long had been deemed impossible for them: significant and sustained economic growth, recently at rates surpassing our own. Too much focus on such external factors, however, can lead us along a path that does not seem best for the future of our innovation system. We would like to emphasize that this book is *not* aimed at regaining U.S. competitive advantage at the expense of other countries. Global competition is an everyday reality but global interaction and collaboration are too. Our concern is not at the relative level of progress between nation states, but at an absolute one: to rebuild an innovation system that has grown ever more inefficient, in light of the paradigm shift that is upon us.

To use Peter Drucker's term, we are firmly in "Post-Capitalism", in which large sums of investment capital, not owned by an individual or necessarily tied to any particular country, are desperately trying to find growth investments. However, the expectations on these investments can only be satiated by a sustained high level of innovation that spurs long-term super-growth. And such super-growth arises from particular *innovation paradigms* that produce expanding, even exponential, benefits.

In the Industrial Revolution, for example, an innovation paradigm was launched that centered upon devices able to convert chemically stored energy into economically useful motion. Why didn't we just say "engines"? Because there were many innovations that involved "engines", from the first steam engines — used in mines and factories, but also soon in boats and in a new mode of transportation, railroads, that transformed societies — to the most advanced jet engines of today. There were also many innovations that devised various ways of creating value from "economically useful motion", from railroads, cars and airplanes to mail-order retail businesses like Sears Roebuck and service businesses like FedEx.

A similar paradigm was the application of electro-magnetism in macroscopic devices, for efficient energy transmission, lighting, radar, radio, television, etc. Here was another interdependent set of fundamental innovations, along with uncountable incremental innovations, combining for tremendous economic and social impact.

We in modern times have been very lucky. Starting in the mid-to-later twentieth century our innovation system created, and our economy thrived upon, the information age paradigm. This paradigm has been driven by Moore's Law, the amazing doubling of transistor density in integrated circuits every two years. And this paradigm is an innovation singularity. It is not often that humankind creates an economic sector in which the base industry — integrated circuits or microprocessors — has super-growth sustained over decades, and multiple industries are built on top of that industry, each having super-growth of its own. These have included personal computers, software, the various Internet industries, mobile telephone systems, embedded sensing and control systems, and more. Not to mention the many industries making components for the devices and systems, at all stages of the numerous supply chains.

This super-growth stemmed not only from the producing industries, but also from the large productivity gains that arose from using products and services directly or indirectly based on Moore's Law. Transistor doubling did more than increase the speed and capacity of microprocessors and the devices they went into. From the end user's viewpoint, the doubling enabled not only faster devices with more memory and storage, but new kinds of devices, and new functionalities. One just has to think back to what the first personal computers or mobile phones were like to realize how great the changes have been. And the same holds true for a much wider array of technologies and applications that use integrated circuits hidden from our view, many of which we depend upon every day for keeping us safe, comfortable and connected. An innovation paradigm like the Moore's Law paradigm is not normal on the scale of centuries.

As with any innovation paradigm, it was inevitable that the impact of Moore's Law would eventually diminish. The increases in the performance of microprocessors have not yet reached their physical limits — indeed, as we shall see, they've been extended by an added fundamental innovation by one of the authors of this book — but these increases have begun to pay diminishing returns in terms of performance gains that make a difference for buyers and users. During the 1980s and '90s, for example, personal computer performance grew by great leaps. First the computers became not only cheap enough, but fast and functional enough, that almost everybody wanted one. Then new machines with new microprocessors kept being noticeably and vastly superior to the older models, one after another. Today, despite continued enhancements to the chips inside, can you truly say that your new computer is a great leap forward from the one before, or is it just somewhat faster, somewhat more powerful? Other limiting factors of many kinds have begun to arise. Ultimately, super-growth depends on delivering super-gains in value to users, and Moore's Law has reached the limit of its capacity to deliver such gains.

But the deeper concern is that the innovation system as a whole has been losing its capacity to generate and deliver fundamental innovations. As we shall show in a later chapter, these innovations take at least 10 to 15 years to have market impact. This means that the super-growth of the 1990s was growth riding mainly on the stored value of innovation processes begun previously. It further seems that while this reaping of the fruits was in progress, not as many new seeds were being planted or new trees cultivated, given that there were fewer fruits to reap through the lean years in the early 2000s. The innovation system that we thought was peaking in the '90s was already entering breakdown. The financial system compounded the damage by creating a series of bubbles, rewarding promises of innovation rather than financing real innovation.

The Moore's Law paradigm is the cocaine that our financial system has grown addicted to. High returns became the expected norm, and when they could no longer be obtained from real innovation-based profit and growth they had to be fabricated somehow to satisfy the demand for them. The distorted valuations during the boom years helped to hide the underlying problem.

Many venture-capital-backed start-up companies were coming on line with "innovations" that showed little hope of earning sustainable profits, but if an IPO could be floated or an acquisition could be swung, there were the big returns.

As we all know, the addiction to these high returns has remained chronic beyond the dot-com and telecom bubbles and has not been limited to venture investors and Wall Street financiers; individual citizens kept demanding the high returns they were used to just the same. Creativity was channeled into manipulation rather than innovation, and the result has been a veritable parade of financial bubbles: the housing-price bubble, its partner the mortgage securities bubble, and the overall derivatives bubble. Meanwhile in the realm of technology investing, capital with high return expectations inflated bubbles in areas such as biotech and cleantech.

And unfortunately, the widespread fixation on financial fantasy goes on masking the real crisis in the innovation system. This system for enabling and supporting innovation has a variety of elements — corporations, universities, government, the private investment community. It is a convoluted sort of "pipeline" that relies heavily on innovators being able to weave their way through and among the various elements as they move through the process of innovating. Perhaps that is inescapably so, but the elements are growing increasingly disjointed and sub-optimal for the purposes they need to serve, hindering progress and sending people down blind alleys. We'll describe these problems more specifically in the later chapters which also suggests guidelines for "Building a New Innovation System".

First, however, we need to show you the details of the innovation process itself. Only by grasping what it is that needs to happen within the system can the various stakeholders get clear insight into how their parts of the system might best be restructured. Viewed through the correct lens, the basic innovation process does not vary much. The same types of steps are required and the same principles are involved regardless of the product, organization or setting.

The following chapters articulate the real innovation process, using examples to show how its basic attributes come into play in diverse cases. Next we'll invite you to follow the true story of a fundamental innovation as it unfolded all the way through the process *and through the winding paths of the innovation system.* We then examine how that system evolved, why it was once so productive, and why it is not any longer. The book closes, as mentioned above, with a forward-looking discussion about what each of us can do. There we speak to each stakeholder in turn, starting with the most important stakeholder in any innovation: the innovator.

Now let's see how real innovation works.

Chapter 2

Inside Real Innovation

"The test of a first-rate intelligence is the ability to hold two opposed ideas in mind at the same time and still retain the ability to function."

F. Scott Fitzgerald
"The Crack-Up", 1936

For much of the twentieth century the magic words were "science" and "technology". People came to see them as the forces driving the progress that we were enjoying, the forces that would go on bringing us an ever better future. But in recent years, "innovation" has become the key word, along with the realization that more fundamental factors are involved.

This chapter presents a conceptual model for explaining and understanding how the innovation process is carried out, *when done optimally*. It is a very simple conceptual model, with only three major elements plus one basic underlying principle. As we shall show with a number of examples, it is also a universal model that can be applied to innovation in any industry and any environment. The model is thus intended to give us not only a clear understanding, but a common language for talking about innovation.

In this context, "innovation" is being used to mean more than ground-breaking research, and more than invention. As important as they are, research and invention are merely parts of a larger whole. We are using "innovation" to mean the entire process of moving new and valuable ideas into the marketplace, where benefits accrue to the users and where return is extracted for investment in the process. In short, we define innovation as *useful embodiments of ideas in the marketplace*.

To understand this process we have to start by putting away a common misconception. The error lies in seeing innovation as a straight-line affair that proceeds roughly as follows:

discovery→invention→development→product→market→profit

Although widely believed, this linear picture does not convey how successful innovation occurs. The linear story of an innovation represents its historical recording, rather than how it was actually generated. Such recordings obscure the true messiness of the process, which can be revealed if original documents have been kept, and if one is able to study them in detail. The work tends to be that of many individuals with complex information exchanges over a period of time. Moreover — and this is the key point — as innovators think and plan, and as they test and develop their ideas, the process is not a "train of thought" that progresses steadily down the track from the lab to the marketplace.

For instance, if you were to spend lot of time and resources developing a research technology into a prototype of a product, and only then begin to address the "implementation" issues such as how you might manufacture and distribute the thing, and then only after *that* start thinking seriously about the market and how much people would value the product, it probably wouldn't be a very good way to proceed. In fact as we shall see more than once in this book, it isn't even a good idea to get locked in regarding any one of the major factors too early in the game. An example would be if you were to assume, on the basis of limited knowledge, that a technology you're developing would be ideal for a particular market sector or end use — and then, without a lot of further checking and constant cross-checking, proceed linearly down that path.

That is not how real innovation, good innovation, works. The process is highly and continuously *iterative.* All three elements — the nature of the product, the implementation into reality, the market to be addressed — are continuously being balanced against each other, and thought of in relation to one another. And typically all elements, or at least the details of them, change as innovation progresses. The process is one of iterating through the elements again and again until they converge, in optimum form, into a product implemented in a market.

Of course decisions and commitments have to be made along the way. The iterative process is not about dithering endlessly. On the contrary, as examples in this book will show, one of its main purposes is to help make the best possible decisions throughout the course of the process. Repeatedly iterating through all the elements of an innovation allows you to see where you really stand at any given point. Blind alleys become evident, as you begin to see how practical constraints in one area rule out certain possibilities in other areas. (To give a very simple example: if an emerging technology would have to violate the laws of physics to meet customer needs in a particular market application, then that application is ruled out, *for that technology*. The question for the next round of iteration then becomes, do we try a different market, or a different technology?)

Repeated iteration also brings the major unknowns and uncertainties into sharper focus, which helps in deciding which options should be kept open and which are better foregone. Innovators encounter frequent but hopefully minor failures. The innovators can then make better informed decisions in choosing when and how to commit resources. Therefore, while the iterative process may look and feel "messy", its real aim is innovation efficiency. When followed diligently it can maximize the chances for success *at every step*, reduce the risk of waste or loss at every step, and give early indication of when a significant change of the innovation course would be advisable.

The same cannot be said for the linear model, which fails when viewed from a simple financial perspective. If we were to follow a truly linear process from left to right,

discovery→invention→development→product→market→profit,

then this implies that we would first have to try out every research idea on the far left before being able to know which ones could result in successful innovations. The same would be true for every invention, and so on, resulting in the all-too-common funnel picture: the winnowing out of winners by brute-force reduction. Given that fundamental innovation requires 10 to 15 years at a minimum to enter the marketplace — and that every stage from left to right requires roughly an order of magnitude higher investment than the one preceding it — then one can determine with a back-of-the-envelope calculation that the investments required for such a funnel could not be afforded.

Yet as later chapters of the book will show, a good bit of money is in fact wasted by chasing what amounts to a "linear funnel model". Public funds are often poured into new research areas, and private funds into new types of start-up companies, with the general expectation that (a) something useful is bound to come out eventually, and (b) the returns on the winners will be high enough to make up for the money lost in funding things that didn't work. We can and must do better all around.

Again, few of us have a mental model of the innovation process that is so simple-mindedly linear as to be laughable. The trouble is that strains of inaccurate linear thinking persist, and they prevent us from understanding how to innovate more effectively. For instance, it is still common to hear discussions of "technology push" versus "market pull". Technology push is said to originate from scientists and engineers trying to push a piece of research or technology onto the marketplace, and it is usually spoken of as a bad force to be avoided. Market pull consists of letting the market dictate, and it is said to be the more enlightened approach: just listen to the call of the customers at the far end of the track, and send them the innovations they want. A person would almost be led to think that taking the right side in this argument is one of the keys to innovation.

In reality, what we are getting here is a pair of linear concepts oversimplified to the point of being useless. To cite an obvious shortcoming, users in a marketplace may not know that they "want" an innovation until it is available. Not many people could even conceive of a personal computer, let alone want one, until the innovation was already well developed. There are countless innovations in which technologists "pushed" the process by anticipating markets rather than merely answering their call. But there is a more basic conceptual error that can mislead us. Technology push vs. market pull is a false dichotomy, a false choice, because the underlying assumptions are incorrect. The innovation process is not a straight line from technology to market. It does not have to be started, or maintained, either by a push from one end or by a pull from the other.

Real innovation more often begins with a confluence of factors coming together in the minds of innovators. They are aware of certain technologies that exist, or could exist; they are also aware of market needs that exist, or they envision uses that could exist. It may be hard to pinpoint where the actual genesis takes place and it hardly matters, for once the process has started, the emerging innovation is liable to be "pushed" and "pulled" in all sorts of directions by events that range from unexpected problems to new ideas. Every twist adds to the multiplicity of choices and trade-offs that one must consider. There is little chance of finding a straight path through this tangle either by pushing technology, or by hoping that clear market signals will shine like a beacon to light the way. The best hope, as we have said, is to iterate repeatedly until the innovation rounds into shape.

A related "linear" misconception is the belief that on the historical scale, basic scientific research must come first, leading to discoveries which then lead to practical applications. The history of technology has seldom progressed in this manner. Ancient smelters and artisans, working empirically, were making fine bronze implements and Damascus steel long before anything was known about the molecular structures of metals. The modern science of metallurgy developed later, with the growing need to make metals more efficiently for more sophisticated uses. In Michael Riordan and Lillian Hoddeson's book *Crystal Fire*,

Gordon Moore, the cofounder and former CEO of Intel, is quoted as having said: "It's not science becomes technology becomes products. It's technology that gets science to come along behind it".

Certainly linear thinking has its proper uses, but why does it persist inaccurately about important matters where there is clear evidence to contradict it? That in itself is an interesting puzzle, the answer to which may have its roots in our human nature as tool users. Whether we used sharp stones mounted on sticks to kill a mammoth or use the Internet today to search for information around the globe, most of our essential tasks in life are accomplished by using tools intentionally to achieve a desired outcome. It is thus only natural that our essential mode of thinking is that of cause and effect. From there, one can then see how linear relations of well defined cause and effect would become hard-wired into our minds, making us prone to cast inherently non-linear processes into linear models.

Unfortunately, such thinking about the innovation process tends to leave us with a muddle of half-truths, untruths and confusing terminology. So let us now proceed with our attempt to clarify the thinking and unify the language by formally presenting a new model of the innovation process. A great deal of complexity can be captured by using a few simple terms, if we define those terms both broadly and precisely.

A New Model of the Innovation Process:
The Three Basic Elements

We have emphasized (indeed, "reiterated") the fact that a good innovation process is highly iterative. We have further said it requires repeated iteration among three key elements, which we shall now formalize by using capital letters: Technology, Market, and Implementation. These three elements can be seen as the basic "factors of innovation" in much the same way that Land, Labor and Capital were once seen as the factors of production.

Before we illustrate the dynamics of iteration, we need to explain more fully what each of the elements consists of. And we can do this by building a bridge of understanding between the old, linear concept of innovation and the new. Keeping in mind that the linear model may have some validity as an after-the-fact recording — but does *not* depict how innovation actually occurs — we reproduce it here one final time:

discovery→invention→development→product→market→profit

Although the process will rarely take place in such an orderly and stepwise fashion, it certainly seems true that everything described in this model is typically *involved* in the process: "development" is done, we eventually wind up with a "product", and so forth. It also certainly seems true that the right-hand side of the line describes the desired end result, and that the items there are fundamentally different from those on the left-hand side. So: remembering, as always, that the process unfolds in iterative loops rather than a straight-line progression, we can roughly map our three elements onto the pieces of the linearized model as follows.

- **Technology** includes the items on the left-hand side. It encompasses those aspects of the innovative idea that are objectively verifiable, by scientific method: all repeatable constructions, formulations, etc. that will eventually make it possible to have an "idea embodied in the marketplace".

- **Market** includes the items on the right-hand side. It encompasses the people who will use the innovation, the benefits they can expect from it, the behaviors they will *change* as they benefit from using the innovation — and the profit they are willing to render to the businesses selling the innovation. Here we are in the realm of so-called human factors, measurable to a degree, but not nearly so predictable or objectively verifiable.

- **Implementation** includes all that must happen to connect the two, moving the Technology of the innovative idea into the human realm of the Market. It encompasses everything required to make the innovation functional in reality, from the forms and methods of production to the forms and methods of delivery.

No distinctions or definitions are immutably perfect. There will of course be gray areas between the elements as we are describing them. But based upon the authors' long collective experience, these three elements are the categories that best and most usefully capture the many different concerns that innovators must address and balance as they go about their creative endeavors.

All will become clearer as we go on to define the elements more succinctly and illustrate them with examples. Let's take each in turn.

Technology includes *any new or old technology that allows the innovative idea to exist and enables it to be executed.* This definition bears a closer look because the term is so easily reduced to oversimplification in everyday use. When a new kind of product first arrives on the marketplace — such as hybrid cars, or the

BlackBerry — people are excited about getting "a new technology". And indeed the product itself is rightly called a technology, in the sense of being a machine, a tool or a device.

But for purposes of understanding the innovation process, Technology with a capital T also includes any and all of the technologies that constitute the innovation. That would include all of the component parts and systems … plus the engineering *designs* for those parts, and for the complete product … *plus* all of the scientific knowledge that had to be acquired and expressed in formulas, equations, computer codes and such, in order for the designs to be made and for the innovative idea to exist in physical form. In the process of developing an innovation, innovators have to pull together this whole kit of stuff called Technology.

An important point, as it says in the definition, is that the technologies may be "new or old". Take a hybrid vehicle, for example. We can surely agree that it is an innovation, but what is the Technology in this innovation? You may say that it is clearly the engine or clearly the battery, but is it possible to design the engine or the battery correctly without taking the braking, ventilation or electrical system into account? "Old" technologies like tires, auto body parts and window glass count, too, because they allow the idea of hybrid *car* to exist and be executed. (For a hybrid train, a different set of existing technologies is used, and the set of new technologies created is different too.) For the hybrid car, you may even go back to the understanding of quantum mechanics, without which it would not have been possible to design the millions of transistors in the control chip that regulates the power distribution. Although the electrical system designer does not have to worry about quantum mechanics, the knowledge is still incorporated within the hybrid vehicle.

Further, many innovations make ingenious re-use of old technologies. The saying "Don't re-invent the wheel" is most apt, because people keep finding new uses for this ancient technology: there is a wheel inside your container of dental floss, and a wheel on the trackwheel computer mouse. We will find that virtually any innovation depends on old technologies as well as new. *In taking an innovation from concept to completion, the "Technology" task is to find and adapt the existing technologies that are useful, and identify and develop the new technologies that are needed.*

We believe this to be a significant definition as it removes the focus on newly contributed technology. Our previous innovation pipeline has focused like a laser beam on newly contributed technology, since the previous paradigm allowed us to efficiently concentrate resources on new technology that seemingly single-handedly created new value, revenue, and return for investors. In reality, this efficient focus was possible because the paradigm made the next product more obvious and contributed many of the required complementary technologies, new and old. Without a strong paradigm going into the new age, we need to include any old technologies so we do not prematurely narrow our chances of innovating successfully.

Moreover, in the definition of Technology we are using, there is no such thing as the difference between a "technology-related" and "non-technology-related" business or innovation. Every innovation throughout history has used technology; every innovation does and will. Here, for example, is what would seem to be an utterly technology-free exception to the rule. A restaurant owner rearranges the tables and chairs in her seating area, thinking it might increase business. She pushes two tables together to make a long one near the plate-glass window in front, so that large groups of people walking by might look in and say, "Hey, here's a place we can all sit together". Some small tables are moved into corners far from the rest to create private nooks; a couple of other changes are made. Sure enough, business picks up. This is clearly an innovation, embodying an idea in useful form in the marketplace, and one could argue there is no technology involved. "This woman is in a service industry and all she did was shuffle some things around to serve her customers better. The tables and chairs don't count as 'technologies' because, um, because she had them already — she didn't add any".

Ah, but the tables and chairs do count. They are existing technologies deployed in a new way. And the new technology she developed, which made the difference, was a technology in her head: the algorithm for table placement. A humble algorithm, to be sure, but it was a logically derived and geometrically expressible set of instructions, executable to achieve a desired effect, and therefore by almost anyone's definition a technology.

Technology includes everything that is objectively verifiable, including all scientific and engineering knowledge, and the algorithm in the head of our restaurant owner. Of course, the vast majority of these can be eliminated from the start as not applicable to a particular innovative idea. But for many innovations, we likely need to cast a wide net for old technologies that can be adapted, and potential new ones that we could create.

Market is defined as *any new or old set of users having a need or desire for the innovation*. We include "old" markets explicitly to remind ourselves not to focus on finding or creating new markets. As with Technology, the old and new are not always clearly distinguishable and any new market is bound to contain elements of old markets. Consider the example of the iPod. On one hand we could argue that the iPod's market was an old market, because people had been listening to portable music of their choice for a long time on their Walkmen or CD players. In that sense we might have expected it be a classic "replacement" market, with the newest manifestation of the idea gradually replacing the existing devices over a period of time — for after all, people have to change their behaviors to use an innovation. To use the iPod they would have to migrate away from their legacy systems, moving their music collections from CDs to mp3 files. By traditional old-market thinking, one would expect this shift to be gradual, much as it was when the original Walkman's cassette tapes were eventually phased out in favor of CDs.

That is not what happened, however. Although the original Walkman had been a tremendous hit, sales of the iPod grew twice as fast, reaching a total of 50 million units in less than five years and then staying at over 50 million units *per year*. Clearly some new market or market behavior was involved, and probably there were several. Perhaps the iPod's added features appealed to people who wouldn't have considered buying a portable music player before. Perhaps the iPod also benefited from coming along later in time, so it could be sold into consumer markets that were more comfortable with advanced electronics and format-switching than those of the previous generation. Or, since the iPod was positioned as a must-have item among children and teens, perhaps many young people wanted one in order to "get" more than the physical product — perhaps all these and more.

For any innovation, evaluating the Market in advance can never be a precise science. But it is important to do it in detail, with a keen eye to factors such as how the nature of the Technology affects the nature of the Market, and vice versa. Also, either or both may *change* during the course of innovating. That is another reason why an ongoing iterative process is required to keep the elements optimally aligned.

One often hears about distinguishing between innovations based on whether they enable customers to do something new, or whether they allow them to do what they are already doing, only better or cheaper. We argue that any *a priori* judgment of markets on such criteria is counterproductive. Any innovation that successfully addresses a real market need or desire will cause a change of human behavior, resulting in an economic or social benefit. The only objective measure is the quantitative assessment of the benefit, reflected in how many people will buy the innovation and how much they are willing to pay. And neither the quantitative parameters nor the optimum target market(s) can be forecast with much certitude at the start of the innovation process. *We thus increase our chances of innovating successfully by keeping our market options as open as possible at the beginning.*

With some innovations, it is fairly clear from the start that they cannot be priced low enough to sell to a mass market, but they can still find profitable niche markets. High-efficiency solar cells are a prime example, as very few of us could afford to cover the roof of a house with these cells, but they are sold into defense and aerospace markets where the performance is worth a premium. What is less noted is that the converse can also occur. Some innovations seem destined to be little more than specialty items at best, yet they find mass-market success. Such was the case with the Walkman. When the first model was released in 1979 there were many skeptics who saw it as a doomed idea from the Market perspective. Here was a portable cassette deck with no microphone or recording head and no built-in speaker, yet it was priced higher than some standard portables which had these "essentials". Who would buy such a thing?

In fact, careful Market thinking had gone into the product's development. Until that time, portable cassette machines were sold primarily to business users and journalists, who used them to record meetings or interviews. The Walkman actually evolved from an earlier product called the Pressman, designed for reporters, but this new innovation had a different Market aim. It was broadly meant for anyone who liked listening to music, and the goal was to provide an ideal yet affordable device for listening while out and about. By the end of the innovation process virtually every feature had been honed to serve that goal. Stripping out the recording function and the speaker allowed the engineers to make a highly compact device, easily carried anywhere, with stereo sound of exceptional quality. Delivering the sound through miniaturized headphones kept the music from bothering others while it also kept ambient noise from interfering with the music. Today this basic design configuration seems obvious. But in the 1970s for Sony, it was a radical departure that grew from being open-minded about whom the Market could consist of, and then ever more focused upon what that Market would want.

Finally, though it should be obvious, we would like to highlight that the potential Markets for innovations are by no means limited to end consumers. A Market may be embedded within an industry supply chain, for example, where the innovation may provide a better or cheaper sub-component, or changes in a manufacturing or delivery process. Such a business-to-business innovation still has to address a need or desire of that market, i.e. the customer's business, and its successful adoption still requires a change in behavior of the people operating that business, whether it is a purchasing manager, a design engineer or a manufacturing line operator. It is not necessary for the customer at the end of the supply chain to benefit directly from the innovation, although this is often the case via either a better or cheaper end product.

Implementation is defined as *any process or knowledge, old or new, used to execute on making the innovation real*. With Technology defined in the realm of the objectively verifiable and Market defined in the human realm, it stands to reason that since Implementation bridges the two, it may have elements in either. Identifying the right business model to bring the innovation to market profitably is one example of Implementation. Industry structures, supply chains, manufacturing processes, market delivery channels, product pricing strategies, business administration structures, etc. all are involved in Implementation.

The legal processes and knowledge used to patent an invention also are translations of Technology into the human realm, in order to protect the invention and, if desired, allow it to be licensed. Thus they too are part of Implementation, because they contribute to making the invention executable in the marketplace. The interactions of Implementation with Technology and Markets are complex. For example, manufacturing may require additional new or old technologies, while delivery channels may need to be changed according to new or old market knowledge.

Although it is impossible to list every item that could constitute Implementation, one quantitative parameter that is vital throughout is cost. A Market's need or desire for an innovation has a finite valuation, i.e., the price it can command. Assessing this in advance may be difficult, but to once again state something that's obvious: Implementation must always deliver the innovation to Market at a cost below its valuation.

Also, while people often think that innovation consists of bringing a new form of Technology to Market, it is possible to have great impact by targeting the Implementation space, and offering a new mode of Implementation. A classic example is that of Morris Chang, the founder of Taiwan Semiconductor Manufacturing Company. Born in Taiwan, Chang moved to the U.S. in the 1950s and lived through the birth and early growth of the semiconductor industry. He joined Texas Instruments in 1958, at the very time when Jack Kilby of that firm co-invented the integrated circuit — the notion of making "chips" with multitudes of transistors and other circuit components etched into them. This of course was a tremendous Technology advance, and one that was quickly built upon.

Meanwhile, Morris Chang's great contribution was yet to come. He rose through the ranks at Texas Instruments, remaining there into the 1980s, by which time TI was one of the world's largest chipmakers. The industry then was still vertically integrated to a high degree. The initial part of the production chain had already begun to be farmed out to materials suppliers, who made the plate-sized silicon "wafers" from which many chips could be made. But then a big firm such as TI would both design the circuitry for the chips, and etch and cut the finished chips from the wafers. The latter part was very expensive. It was repetitive but high-precision work that required a fabrication line, or "fab", costing in the vicinity of a billion dollars.

Chang noticed that at TI alone, there were chip designers with more new ideas, for more potential markets, than could be accommodated on the company's fab lines. Some groups of these designers had left the firm to work independently, and were searching for manufacturers willing and able to produce their designs. Chang saw that this could be a useful business in its own right. Returning to Taiwan for an industrial-development position that enabled him to raise the needed investment, he launched Taiwan Semiconductor Manufacturing Company (TSMC) as the world's first major "silicon foundry", a dedicated producer of chips for designers.

The foundry was loaded with complex equipment but very little new Technology had to be developed. TSMC devoted itself to the Implementation of new Technology ideas from others. And it transformed a global industry. As TMSC earned profits and other silicon foundries sprung up, the entry barrier for everyone with new chip designs was lowered dramatically. You didn't need your own fab line; you only needed enough capital to start a "fabless semiconductor company" — of which there are now multitudes worldwide, designing many of the chips for products that we all use every day, and having them made on a contract basis at foundries like TSMC.

The point of the story is simple. Implementation matters tremendously. With so much attention being paid to new Technology and the cultivation of new Markets, it is easy to forget that Implementation can make all the difference in the world.

One final note: since Implementation includes all business processes required for delivering an innovation to market, we should clarify the relationship between Implementation and entrepreneurship. Implementation does not require entrepreneurship because only a subset of innovations is brought to market by new companies. The past 15 years of venture capital unjustifiably associated innovation Implementation with entrepreneurship, a conflation that doesn't do justice to either activity. Entrepreneurs are vitally important to any economy. In many cases, a new firm is the only entity suited for bringing a particular innovation to market, and one must also remember that every existing company was once a start-up: none would exist if entrepreneurs had not started them.

However, some innovations require resources beyond the capacity of a start-up, such as very large investment or market access, and many incremental innovations are carried out by existing businesses. Although a start-up company that achieves real profitability will have successfully executed on some degree of innovation, most of the innovation process has likely been performed prior to company formation. Successful entrepreneurship requires tapping into innovation as the final stages of the innovation process are supported during the entrepreneurial phase. We shall discuss this overlap in subsequent chapters, but for the sake of this definition, Implementation shall not imply entrepreneurship or vice versa.

The Iterative Process

Having gotten acquainted with the three basic elements of innovation, we turn to the process of iterating through them. For any innovation — and you are welcome to imagine any one that you like — we need to find the right pieces of Technology that, when Implemented in just the right way, meet the right Market needs for turning our innovative idea into a profitable business. So how does one iteratively go about getting everything "just right"?

This can become very complicated so we are going to explain and illustrate it, successively, in four different ways:

- First, with a little analogy that compares the innovation process to a more familiar problem-solving activity that nearly all of us have tried.
- Next, with a step-by-step description of iterative innovation. The description is given in general, conceptual terms but it is rigorous.
- Then, in this chapter and the following one, with three hypothetical cases. These are drawn from real life, but they are simplified by combining and/or fictionalizing parts of various stories. The purpose is to show you streamlined versions of the process in action.
- Finally, in Chapter 5, we will delve into the actual case history of a fundamental innovation, with all of the flavor and details of the true story.

In the course of this journey we will also be fleshing out the bigger picture, to prepare for the final chapters in which we discuss the American innovation *system* and how it supports — or fails to support — the iterative innovation process. But let us not look too far ahead; first we need a clear picture of the process.

In the examples of innovations that we have used thus far, such as the iPod, the Walkman, and TSMC, the stories were greatly abbreviated in order to make specific points about the elements of the innovation process. We barely touched on the multiple iterations that were required to bring these ideas into their final form. To convey the magnitude of the iterative task, we start with our analogy.

Iterative innovation is like building a giant jigsaw puzzle. Suppose that you have recently given birth to an innovative idea. You've now come home with your puzzle kit in a box. The picture on the lid of the box, showing how the assembled puzzle ought to look, corresponds to your initial notion of what the completed innovation might look like when it is delivered to the marketplace as part of a profitable business. This picture will be your guideline for starting out, and it is a beautiful scene from nature.

In the foreground is bright and lively meadow. That's your Technology: all of the new and old technologies that will bloom together, allowing your innovative idea to exist and enabling it to be executed.

On the horizon is a dense forest. That's the Implementation: all of the new and old processes and knowledge you may use to execute on making the innovation real.

Glowing above the meadow and the forest is a blue sky. That's the Market, of course: every new or old set of users that will have a need or desire for the innovation.

We said it was a big puzzle. To put things in order, you empty out the pieces and, by looking at the colors, sort them into three buckets: one each for Technology, Implementation and Market. There appear to be thousands of pieces in each bucket. You can already appreciate that it will be impossible to build such a large puzzle in a linear fashion. Instead you will need to try a lot of pieces to see if they fit, put them aside, try the next ones you think likely to fit, and so on.

However, the innovation process is much more complicated than that. One challenge is that the buckets initially contain many more puzzle pieces than you can use. This is only natural, because in the early stage of an innovation, no one can be sure exactly which pieces of Technology, Implementation and Market will work best together, so it's good to start with a range of possibilities. You can eliminate some of the pieces quickly by figuring out that they don't belong in this picture. But you are still left with a sizable number that seem "too close to call" — you can't yet tell whether you will need them or not.

A second challenge is that your guiding puzzle picture on the box lid is not well defined at all. Since it is just an idea, it's very fuzzy, especially at the borders between Technology, Market and Implementation. That is disconcerting, as a normal puzzle would have the sharpest contrast at the section borders. A normal puzzle picture also wouldn't have the alarming property of seeming to shift and waver, giving you the queasy feeling that portions of the picture have changed size or moved since the last time you looked.

A third and most significant challenge is that the shapes of many of your puzzle pieces are also not very well defined. They may have the right colors and patterns to go with other pieces that would be their logical neighbors, but their shapes are such that they won't pop into place. Worse yet, there appear to be none of the valuable "framing" pieces that have a straight side or a square corner. These are the pieces that go along the outside edges of the picture, allowing you to frame and constrain the problem, as it were, and making it easier to fill in the rest. Without a clear-cut frame, you can't even tell what the boundaries of this project are!

The puzzle pieces of ill-defined shape might be the way they are for a couple of reasons. Some represent items that you don't fully understand, and perhaps when you learn more about them you will see that they fit, or perhaps they won't fit. Others are "raw" pieces, such as undeveloped technologies, which you might be able to mold into the desired shapes — although only to a certain degree, and not arbitrarily.

All of these additional challenges correspond to the inherent uncertainties in Technology, Market and Implementation, as well as in the innovative idea, when we start an innovation process. This is why the process is far more than a combinatorial task, although the combinatorial aspect by itself is usually pretty daunting.

The keys to our ability to innovate despite the challenges are **learning** and **abstraction**. These two human capabilities give the uncertainties a second face, creating the freedom we need for possibly arriving at the functional outcome we seek. The innovation process iteratively and repeatedly invokes these two capabilities. Our "fuzzy" initial innovative idea is an abstraction of what could be. Even on this rough abstract level, we can ask about critical features that the possible technologies, implementations and markets possess, to get a sense of whether an innovation based on our idea could conceivably exist and work.

This initial feasibility assessment is where the rounds of iteration begin. We first want to turn to the element (Market, Implementation, or Technology) we perceive to pose the greatest risk for our innovative idea at the start, which is equivalent to turning to the category having the greatest uncertainty — either because we don't understand enough about it or because nobody does. In either case, we now have to learn about the components in this category and how they could fit together to exhibit the rough characteristics we need in the context of our innovative idea. Returning to the jigsaw-puzzle analogy, this is like laying out the puzzle pieces that could belong to one part of the picture and taking stock of whether we think that there are enough pieces overall: ideally, there should be more than we think ultimately necessary. If there aren't, then we need to see if we can find additional pieces by searching beyond the boundaries initially considered. We also need to learn the shapes of the pieces better, and estimate to what extent which pieces are pliable, in order to get an idea of whether a satisfactory fit could be achieved.

With this increased understanding — but without actually building the section — we then abstract our learning to a range of characteristics that this category could exhibit. Having narrowed the uncertainty of this category, we deliberately switch our attention to the category which we perceive to have the next most uncertainty, and then to the final category. Repeating the learning and abstraction processes for these categories, we can decide whether our innovative idea is *conceivable*, i.e., whether it could exist at all.

Having increased our knowledge through learning about individual pieces, and having increased our confidence through abstraction that we could achieve characteristics for producing a fit, we then continue the learning and abstraction processes, iterating again through Technology, Market and Implementation. This time, we pay more attention to the sub-sections in each category and whether we think they too can be made to fit together. With this further increased knowledge and confidence about our innovative idea, we can decide whether it is *feasible* and thus worthwhile to pursue further.

Throughout this process, we will find it necessary to modify our innovative idea and adapt it to our learning to maximize the options for success. Continued iterations of increasingly refined learning and increasingly refined abstraction of characteristics, while adjusting the innovative idea, will either lead us to conclude that a successful outcome is impossible, or it will make the success of our innovation first possible, then probable, then more probable, and so on. This continued process of learning and abstraction to reduce risk and increase the chance of a positive outcome constitutes the non-linear iterative innovation process. It maximizes the return on innovation.

In contrast, a focused development in one category while delaying the others and expecting them to fit together sometime later does not make full use of the freedom which iterative learning and abstraction allow. Failing to iterate through Technology, Market and Implementation from the beginning will likely result in trying to fit a square peg into a round hole. Note that what we've just said is opposed to common understanding. Advances in Technology are thought to develop in a sort of R&D vacuum, without any input until a fortuitous discovery or invention is made; then Market and Implementation are explored. Since there are an infinite number of science and technology interests to be explored, the probability of actually working on the right problem (i.e. one that results in a successful innovation) without other inputs is vanishingly small.

The nature of the learning that is required changes as we move through the iterative innovation process. At the beginning, our learning needs to be broad. We're trying to get an overview of which old and new technologies, which old and new markets and which old and new implementation knowledge and processes we ought to consider for maximizing the chances of a feasible innovation. We also need to quickly fill in the holes in our knowledge, to sufficient depth that we can accurately abstract the relevant characteristics and assess the corresponding risks. This can often be done by absorbing and correlating existing knowledge found in scientific literature and market studies, as well as analysis of the operating and financial characteristics of comparable industries. Extrapolations based on such existing data, along with good back-of-the-envelope calculations, often serve the feasibility assessment well enough and allow for a rapid, low-cost turnaround.

As we progress further into the process, more in-depth learning is required. If the innovation involves new technologies, markets and/or implementations, we will obviously need to build some new knowledge by using experimental methods in the relevant areas. Scientific lab experiments, prototyping, manufacturing simulations, quantitative business analyses and direct market studies are just a few of the possible methods.

But more important and often neglected, especially during the early stages of innovation, is the "experimental" learning needed about the *relationships* between Technology, Market and Implementation. Based on our innovative idea, we tend to have our own assumptions about many things: not only how the Technology could be desired by a Market, but how the Technology could be implemented and what form it should take, what the relation between Implementation cost and Market valuation could be, or what Market delivery constraints could exist. Yet existing data is rarely available for evaluating the relevant cross-category relations. Insight can often be gained only through *direct transactional experiences*, which usually involve talking to people. For example, a conversation with a manufacturing manager about whether he is concerned about such-and-such, and to what extent he would value a corresponding improvement, could quickly reveal whether certain assumptions about an innovative idea are roughly correct or off-base. It is always more likely than not that our assumptions are wrong, and the direct feedback will either invalidate the innovative idea early, or redirect it towards where the real value is.

We use the term "transactional experiences" instead of something like "asking for opinions" because, as the time grows ripe, potential and actual transactions will be at stake in these exchanges. Instead of asking possible users if they would see value in an innovation, we might be asking them to take part in field-testing a pilot version. Talks with possible suppliers will get to the point of discussing details about producing parts or delivering services, and so forth. The goals at any stage are *to solicit feedback that is genuine rather than merely speculative*, and *to resolve as much uncertainty as possible with minimal commitment of one's resources or those of others*. Ultimately, the experiences we have during the process of negotiating real contracts with potential suppliers or customers — for example, for the delivery of test batches in the context of a joint development agreement — provide some of the most real and instructive feedback. The spirit, as always, is to move forward iteratively but with real purpose.

Two Hypothetical Cases

With a conceptual description of the iterative innovation process in hand, we can now illustrate a couple of different ways it might be carried out. Following are hypothetical examples from two very different industries. The first one features a hypothetical person you have met. Remember our restaurant owner?

By altering the layout of her restaurant, she has increased revenue. (Which is far from unheard-of in this industry, by the way. The whole coffee-shop phenomenon, pioneered by Starbucks and others, was based not on selling coffee but on giving the patrons a congenial setting.) At any rate, our restaurant owner is eager to explore new frontiers. Her small-town establishment along Route 66 has been optimized to suit the preferences of the customers in that area. It is by far the most popular restaurant in town, but though it is doing well, the business has matured. The far-reaching new ideas that keep bubbling up in the owner's head cannot be tried in the current location, so they remain ideas rather than innovations. Innovations require experimenting with greater uncertainty in Technology, Market and Implementation.

The owner cuts her own pay in order to hire a manager, keeping the current restaurant and business model incrementally evolving. She knows there are potential markets in the larger urban area 50 miles away. But she does not know those markets *exactly* as she has never executed in them before, so she reads trade literature and talks with friends in the business, until she has acquired enough useful information to get a basic start in this new locale. Still, there are a number of unknowns regarding particular things that she would like to try. For instance, some of her menu items in the original restaurant are unique to the rural market — could they be popular with the urban crowd? She also wonders about some other items, and finding the culinary skills to prepare them.

Renting a space in the city, she sets up the new restaurant according to the layout that has worked so well in the rural area, but with some changes that she has learned may be crucial here. She introduces a hostess concept and parking arrangements more in line with urban expectations. She times the waiters and waitresses to make sure that patrons are getting prompt attention. For some of the new arrangements her assumptions are spot-on, and for some she needs to adjust and modify. She has brought over one of her most experienced cooks from the rural restaurant, and some of his primary menu features are filling a real niche in the new market, as she had hoped.

Although she quickly builds a loyal crowd of regulars who come for these special menu items, the restaurant operation seems to divide into an overly-busy two-hour evening period and times when her staff and set-up are significantly underutilized. She realizes that this gap has to do with happy hours elsewhere and early dining, so she hires a short-order cook who is skilled in catering to these needs. She urges the creation of new menu items for the early dining crowd, a distinct market which somehow she had been unaware of, despite her previous research. After some initial difficulties, the rural chef and the short-order cook interact to create an outstanding early-dining menu with a unique city/country balance. This does more than fill the gap in the revenue stream; it becomes the restaurant's biggest attraction.

Meanwhile the owner has recognized that her initial choice of location was not optimal, although it is good enough to be quite profitable now. So with her growing knowledge of big-city markets, she leases space in a better location for a second urban restaurant. That one also does well, though it requires some additional tweaking for differences in the types of clientele: for instance, take-out meals are popular in the new neighborhood. Finally, with multiple restaurants and the promise of more growth to come, the owner finds that she needs to run her entire operation more efficiently than before. This turns out to be accomplished in a number of ways. New equipment helps, both in the urban locations and in the original rural restaurant. Some further shuffling of key staff members and responsibilities among the various locations achieves a smoother-running mix of personnel, as well as an exchange of creative ideas. Also, with many common items in the restaurants, the supply chain changes. Restaurants that had essentially been a small string of islands are becoming parts of a true enterprise.

With that story a rousing success, let us consider a second example. This case is likewise fictionalized, but rooted in experiences that are all too real. Our innovator is a PhD student at MIT. A product of the best undergraduate and graduate programs in the U.S., he develops a new solar cell that has an eye-opening efficiency of 50%. Most deployed solar cells today are between 10% and 20% efficient. The student is supremely excited and the venture capitalists roaming the hallways are excited, too. Estimates are made, based on what the university's fabrication process can be like in production volumes, and high-tech executives from other industries are hired since they have start-up experience and the student does not. With much fanfare, a company is launched.

At first, everything appears to be on target. Scaling up the university operation is going well. Customers are interested, as the members of the start-up company are informally discussing 50% efficient cells at the cost of the current ones. However, as the technology is scaled, they realize that certain assumptions do not hold. In addition, customers are requiring particular characteristics besides 50% efficiency that are incompatible with the way the solar cells are made. Moreover, the main customer ends up being a company that erects solar cells on roofs, and all current suppliers deliver standard modules with the solar cells fully integrated. These are skills and technology that the company does not have.

After altering the manufacturing process and applying resources to the making of modules, the first cells to be sold are more expensive and only 30% efficient. The original customer, who had bought trial versions of the university solar cells, now has other options in the marketplace, and chooses not to buy the production cells. The good news is that another company is very interested in the production cells, because they are lighter than other cells that have 30% efficiency. But the new customer requires yet different features, requiring more changes to the manufacturing process. At last, after seven years and much more capital than investors or the graduate student had imagined, the company becomes cash-flow positive and the future is bright.

Both of the above fictional anecdotes show success through the iterative innovation process. In the restaurant case, the significant innovation was creating a stable new restaurant business in the city, which could then be built upon as a platform for further growth. Repeated iterations across Technology, Market and Implementation were used, with different components of each coming into play — and into interplay with one another — at different stages. In the initial round, the urban Market was sized up, and Technology was deployed accordingly — with a mixture of old and new algorithms for restaurant layout and operation, as well as some old and new menu items. This was done within an Implementation framework that included renting the location, hiring and monitoring new staff, and transferring one old staff member: the chef from the rural location.

Much tweaking and adjusting then occurred in later rounds, as uncertainties and unknowns were gradually resolved. A significant unknown surfaced in the Market realm, the matter of the early-dining crowd. This was dealt with both through Implementation (hiring the short-order cook, and then having him interact with the rural chef) and eventually through new Technology (the new early-dining menu that was a hit). In all areas there were micro-failures and difficulties along the way, and not all were headed off at zero to little cost through mental learning and abstraction. The "transactional experiences" that produced the learning and removed the uncertainties came at some cost, through trial and error in the course of operating. However, none of them involved a truly costly plunge in a wrong direction. As we said earlier, that is a primary benefit of correctly iterating *the relationships between all three elements* — Technology, Market, and Implementation — from the very start. Clearly that was what the restaurant owner did, as we saw her constantly striving to bring the elements into alignment.

The solar cell case did not start off so well in that respect. Here we had a brilliant inventor but a naïve innovator in the PhD student. He and his investors seemed to fall into the classic error of becoming overly entranced with the Technology. Significant early commitments were made on the basis of just *one aspect* of Technology (the promise of 50% efficiency), with the main learning and abstraction being an estimate of how the fabrication process would scale. Although the solar Market appeared to be a sure thing, actual transactions with this Market revealed it had many sub-markets with varying needs and demands. More troubling yet, in the first transactional contacts after the company was formed, the offer that was floated to the Market turned out to be one the company couldn't deliver on (that same 50% efficiency, at low cost).

There also turned out to be unwelcome surprises in the Implementation area, from problems in scaling the process to learning that a key customer would want his solar cells delivered in integrated modules. As a result of the various oversights, substantially more capital was burned than anyone had expected. To the company's credit, however, the innovators got back on track and were soon iterating across Technology, Market and Implementation to meet the flurries of unexpected requirements. Although the innovation did not perform as initially hoped, the "lower" efficiency of 30% was still very good. The company became cash-positive with strong future prospects, a milestone that many high-tech start-ups never reach. In the end, uncertainties were identified and resolved without sinking what could be a very impactful, and profitable, innovation.

A Diagrammatic View

The stories above are fictitious but in terms of the kinds of challenges faced, and how iterative innovation is applied to produce useful outcomes, they are truer to life than most journalistic and historical accounts of innovations.

Let's assume that the solar cell innovation results in a major market success. How will it be recorded? It will be made linear, something like the following. MIT student discovers key solar technology; key investment and management identified the right market; $X value was created. Although informative at some level, such a recording does not reveal the workings of the real innovation process.

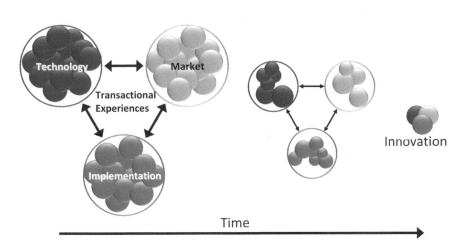

Figure 1: Innovation requires constant iteration between Technology, Market and Implementation. The more fundamental the innovation, the more uncertainty in each category, and therefore the longer it takes to converge on the final embodiment of the innovation.

We try to capture the iterative innovation process in the schematic in Figure 1. Technology, Market and Implementation each contain a large array of pieces and options that could conceivably contribute to turning an idea into a real innovation. The sizes of circles are an indication of the uncertainty that remains in each category at a given stage of the process. Large uncertainty means high risk but also many options. For example, the Technology circle is large when we are furthest from the end-market innovation, and is composed of a large number of "globes" in Fig. 1. We can think of these globes as pieces of fundamental science, or new or old pieces of technology. The initial uncertainty in each category depends on the nature of the innovative idea. Incremental innovations start with less uncertainty and take less time to complete, while fundamental innovations are characterized by much uncertainty in all three categories at the beginning of the process. As we iterate through Technology, Market and Implementation, our learning in each category and especially our learning about fits and misfits between the categories, which we gain efficiently through transactional experiences, continuously reduces risk and increases the probability of a successful outcome. As the number of globes within each circle is reduced, it means that options are being *removed* from the equation because they have been tested and *failed*. Sequential failures of the Technology, Market and Implementation pieces of innovation are required to supply feedback into the other categories.

As Technology, Market and Implementation mutually depend on each other, the solution can only be found by iterating between these factors, improving the embryonic innovation progressively. If the failures are kept small enough and learning from the failures occurs fast enough from a financial perspective, the innovation happens. If not, the potential innovation and the funding enterprise may fail. Thus, innovation requires sequential failure but with lessening severity, eventually converging on an optimal implementation of something truly new.

This innovation process model does not depend, in its formulation, on any particular environment or other factors that nurture the process. A distinct difference in our approach is that we are defining the core innovation process first at the ground level. The macro-environment and "nutrients" that aid or interfere with the innovation process can change with time. Most other works on innovation do not have this level of resolution on the innovation process, and therefore they tend to concentrate on symptoms or on the effects of the macro-system prevalent at the time (e.g. venture capital financing), which prevents us from understanding the core elements of innovation itself.

To use an analogy, the iterative innovation process of Fig. 1 is equivalent to describing the biochemical processes that make a tree grow. If we were to concentrate on the effects of water, soil, air, etc., as other works on innovation tend to do, we could certainly establish some relationships between those "nutrients" and tree growth, but this would actually tell us nothing about the nature of the tree and how it grows. By understanding the tree itself first, we can later establish the effect of different nutrient combinations much more accurately.

The next chapter will deepen the picture of the core process, and also broaden it. We will consider the personal qualities that an innovator needs to develop and use, and add some detail to show how they can be turned to good effect in just one round of iteration.

Chapter 3

One Person, One Iteration at a Time

For many years in the past, when great work was done in any field, the prevailing view was that it was done by geniuses who simply had special gifts or qualities that most of us do not. In modern times we take a more nuanced view. It does seem evident that certain people have certain aptitudes that make them particularly well suited to play music, or perform surgery — or innovate. But it is also clear that many human capabilities can be nurtured and developed, then combined with practical knowledge to perform any number of tasks more effectively.

We shall focus here on the mix required for iterative innovation. We'll show how one innovator, bringing an optimum combination of skills and knowledge into action, can revise and advance an idea substantially in a single round of iteration. That focus on the individual innovator will then lead us into some observations about innovation teams and good environments for innovating. However one must keep returning to the fact that it is people who innovate, not environments or systems, and each person matters.

In general, we could agree that the innovation process requires a person to be "creative". What does that mean, exactly? Obviously it means imagining what could be, as opposed to dwelling upon what is. It also means something beyond the kind of unbounded imagination that's just unproductive daydreaming. A more precise description of the kind of creative thinking we're looking for would be: "envisioning possibilities in the context of practical realities, while projecting into a future. filled with uncertainties, and choosing how to proceed for a desired result".

That sounds like a lot to ask of a person, and it is. Innovation is difficult. The description implies that a person who becomes a narrowly thinking specialist of any type may have trouble innovating successfully. In fact, it suggests that both breadth and depth are equally important, as breadth is essential for "envisioning possibilities" and depth is essential for doing so "in the context of practical realities". The "well-roundedness" that is called for involves the mental agility to *learn and process what one needs to know* across the relevant areas of Technology, Market and Implementation. This can be mastered by a person of reasonable aptitude who has the intelligence to cultivate both a prepared mind, and presence of mind.

Our single-innovator example will now show how such mastery can pay off. As in the previous chapter, we are constructing here a fictionalized, composite portrait of an innovator, and we are placing her in a type of situation with which the authors have had much personal experience.

The innovator is an engineer, working at a technology-and-manufacturing firm. Although her work is satisfying, she has been looking for a significant innovative idea on which she can take the lead, and build it into an innovation brought to market by a start-up venture. Recently she has found what looks like the right idea. It came to her from a friend in a related industry. The friend works at a company that builds a popular critical-equipment system, and he was complaining about a certain component which is the bottleneck of the whole system. The method of producing this component today has a very low yield and is therefore very expensive. Furthermore, the component's performance variability causes high testing costs during system assembly. If there were a way to address the low yield and performance stability problems, it could even open up the design window for the system.

Our innovator thinks she sees a way. Being somewhat familiar with this type of component, which is indeed notorious, she is able to quickly get some additional details from her friend and other sources about the design of the thing and the nature of its misbehavior. Sure enough, it appears there might be a cheaper way of making a better component.

An initial feasibility assessment is in order. At this point, our innovator cannot know or understand all the practical pieces of Technology, Market and Implementation that could be relevant to her idea, but she can learn. She concentrates on the area which she perceives has the greatest initial risk, Technology, and tries to figure out what she needs to take into account. In order not to waste time and money reinventing the wheel, she needs to find most, if not all, existing technologies that could contribute to producing the characteristics she envisions for her innovation. A couple of those she knows quite well, from her industry experience, but there are others. Her engineering background allows her to think of ways these other characteristics can be achieved and for which other applications they could be useful.

She reviews the specifications of relevant technologies and applications in competing, adjacent and complementary industries, and she analyzes what is available through the various supply chains. Although she cannot get all the information she would like, this is good enough for now. With her engineer's understanding, she can extrapolate from what she does know to assess the relevance of the existing Technology pieces to first order. However, there are some additional pieces she thinks are needed which do not seem to exist anywhere, and she is confident that this is not because she missed them.

Could those pieces be designed and made? Drawing now on the science part of her education, she goes back to first principles and calculates whether or not the missing characteristics could be achieved without violating natural laws or being off by orders of magnitude. Of course, she does not remember all the equations offhand, but she finds them in her old textbooks. Her calculations are not entirely accurate, because more accuracy would come at the cost of more detailed work and require information she doesn't have, but they show that there is clearly room to maneuver. She can already see that some parts are going to be really tough to get to work, if at all, but that is for later.

Confident that the Technology analysis provides enough options, and that there are no absolute show-stoppers, she decides to move to the Market side as this area seems the next riskiest. The move is difficult to make, mentally, because she has gained some momentum on the Technology side and has ideas on how to dig deeper. But that must wait.

Despite sales experience during the course of her career, she has no first-hand knowledge of this Market. To check the Market assumptions she has made, she had better learn directly. Who is the customer? Well, of course it's a company like the one her friend works for; in fact that very company is the prime prospect. But who in such a company? She talks with her friend and together they identify the decision makers and persons who would have to change their behavior if the innovation were used: the VP Technology, the Director of Quality Assurance, the Director of System Design, and the Purchasing Manager. Her friend arranges a meeting with the VP Technology.

Having worked in a sales function, our innovator has developed good customer interaction and negotiation skills. She understands how technical component purchasing decisions rely on engineering, commercial and legal factors. Desiring some protection for her innovative idea, and in order to establish an initial level of trust, she asks for a mutual Non-Disclosure Agreement before the meeting. She signs it because it is pretty much standard and she has seen many like it before.

During the meeting with the VP Technology, the Purchasing Manager is also present. There is no need for her to divulge any details of her technical thinking, as she has abstracted the characteristics so that she can describe how they would address the customer's cost problem related to the component. The conversation goes smoothly because she can talk on the interest level of both managers. Influenced by the Purchasing Manager's presence, the VP Technology likes what he hears, but suggests that our innovator talk with the Director of Quality Assurance and the Director of System Design.

Although there still is no need to reveal the core of her innovative idea, this second meeting goes into more detail of system cost and performance. Our innovator learns that the quality assurance protocol is really more integrated with other system components than she had thought, and she senses reluctance from the Quality Assurance Director to change it. Furthermore, the QA protocol has been fine-tuned to accommodate the variability of the current component in relation to others. Any reduction in purchasing cost the company would enjoy from her innovative new component would likely be offset by an increase in cost for developing and establishing a new quality assurance protocol that affects many other components. Worse, changing the QA protocol would need to be communicated to the buyers of the entire system, and if this were not to go smoothly, it could affect their sense of trust in the reliability of the overall system, which is a risk that management probably would not go for.

Our innovator's idea is starting to look dead in the water. Then comes one of those moments that illustrate the truth of the saying, "Chance favors the prepared mind". In a remark on the side to his colleague, the Director of System Design mentions that a larger scale system — something the company has been wanting to design and sell, to grow its own markets — would require a new test protocol. Our innovator picks up on this comment and quickly performs an estimate in her head. The current component is not scalable. Her innovative component can be scalable because of the same piece of Technology that would make it less expensive. Sensing a possibility, she gently steers the conversation towards larger systems and where the industry is headed. Because of the Non-Disclosure Agreement in place, the Director of System Design acknowledges that they are making efforts to develop a larger system, and the first company that would achieve that would have a big competitive advantage. So before talking to the VP Technology again, our innovator needs to investigate the Implementation possibilities, as her innovative idea has just been shifted due to Market feedback.

Her previous ideas of how she could manufacture the component and how she could run the business have been upset by the Market shift. Whereas before she planned on outsourcing about 90% and making the most critical 10% herself, she now cannot do that because no supply chain exists for outsourcing 90% of the parts of a scaled-up, larger component. Can she tap into another supply chain? During her prior search for existing Technology pieces, she came across some at much larger scale in a different industry, too large even for the new component size being envisioned. She hadn't pursued those further, but had kept notes on them. She knows that technologically, they can be scaled to the size she needs, but can she find existing suppliers who will make and sell them to her? She needs to learn about their manufacturing processes and business models to put together a new supply chain.

Speaking with sales people across several companies, she finds that most are quite willing to sell her the sizes she needs at a reasonable price, but there are two pieces that current manufacturers are not willing to scale to her need at the quantities she desires. After investigating the manufacturing process and the production equipment involved, she finds that scaling to her needs is possible if one scales the production equipment accordingly. Luckily, the equipment she would need is mostly custom-made and the equipment manufacturers are quite willing to build it to her specifications. But that is expensive. After learning about the manufacturing processes of the pieces she needs, she puts together a new supply chain where she can outsource about 70%, but in addition to her 10% of critical technology, she now needs to build a manufacturing infrastructure for the remaining 20%, with high equipment cost. This upsets her original business model and idea of cost reduction.

So how much would the new and larger component cost, altogether, and would that be below the Market valuation in order to allow for a profit? She obtains equipment quotes from the suppliers and estimates the operating cost. She can quickly put together a rough model of fixed and variable costs because of accounting courses she took in college, and because she has some idea about equipment financing from her industry job. All in all, after her first pass at scaling and cost modeling, it seems that she will not have a great cost advantage, but didn't the Director of System Design say that *their* competitive advantage would be huge with a larger system? So maybe if she were to patent not only her original 10% piece of technology, but also the equipment design and process of making the additional 20% that she cannot outsource any more, that would make for a pretty strong patent portfolio protecting her new component.

She needs to ask the VP Technology if they would be willing to invest in a company that could ultimately result in exclusivity for them to produce the larger system. And if they were willing to invest in her company to de-risk the potential innovation, would they perhaps then want to buy the company at the pilot production stage if it succeeds? That would mean that she wouldn't have to raise high-interest money in a start-up for the production build-out, but could concentrate on her innovation with probably a better return for herself. This would be a completely different strategy from what she envisioned before. But before she can have that conversation with the VP Technology, she needs to figure out how well she can scale her own 10% technology piece to the new requirements.

Despite the roller-coaster ride through the uncertainties of her first iteration of the innovation process, our innovator feels energized by the opportunity of enabling a whole new system. She rolls up her sleeves and dives deeper into technological details with much enthusiasm, while reflecting on how much time and money she would have wasted if she had failed to iterate early. But now she is on the right track as she starts the next iteration of the innovation process.

A Closer Look at How the Thinking Works

While we leave our innovator to her second round, let's have a closer look at the skills she invoked for successfully performing the first iteration through Technology, Market and Implementation. Although she did not possess the majority of relevant knowledge in any of the three categories, she managed to efficiently learn what she needed. Her engineering background and practical experience in industry enabled her to assess the relevance of existing Technology pieces and identify missing ones. Her science background allowed her to perform quick calculations on the feasibility of whether the missing Technology pieces could exist. Her industry sales experience, business communication skills and knowledge of good practices, like proactively signing the Non-Disclosure Agreement, set her up for learning about the Market needs directly from the customer. And her combined engineering and business skills — including a bit of accounting knowledge and a good sense for manufacturing realities — let her devise a new potential supply chain. With some understanding of patent strategy added in, she had a new business strategy.

Her interdisciplinary background and practical experience in how science and technology work, fundamentally, and in how humans fundamentally operate in business settings, were thus quintessential enablers for learning what she needed. Her learning efficiency certainly correlates with the strength of her interdisciplinary background, but it also depends on her ability to absorb diverse information quickly. Her learning firmly anchored her innovation activity in the practical realities of Technology, Market and Implementation.

Equally important was her ability to abstract from her learning. When she performed the back-of-the-envelope scientific calculations, she could abstract the results to judge that there is probably enough room to maneuver and did not get hung up on the details. Similarly, she abstracted her learning on Technology components to judge that there are likely enough options without having to characterize every single one in detail, and she could abstract the technical and performance characteristics to have effective conversations with the business and engineering folks at the potential customer company. Her abstraction of manufacturing processes enabled her to talk to potential suppliers and develop a sufficiently accurate cost model. All these abstractions served the crucial function of being able to *communicate* across the categories of Technology, Market and Implementation, whether in the real conversations with her potential customer and suppliers or in the conversations she was having in her own mind.

The ability to abstract also made the learning more efficient, because the guiding questions for what she needed to learn next were derived from her abstractions. From 30,000 feet, one can assess the topography of a landscape and identify the blank spots, but one needs to drop down to the ground level to do the actual surveying. The more quickly one can go back and forth between ground-level and bird's-eye views, the more guided and efficient the learning process will be.

A further critical skill of our innovator was her ability to make high quality decisions in the face of uncertainty. Moving from Technology to Market just as she understood the Technology components better, reconstituting her innovative idea after Market transactions shattered her original one, then pressing on to establish a new supply chain and reformulate her business model, all required not just resilience, but active confidence to *head straight in the direction of uncertainty*. Perceiving uncertainty as opportunity rather than being intimidated by it is related to the psychological fabric and inherent personality of a human being. But the confidence to actively engage uncertainties head-on is built upon experiences of having successfully reduced risk by repeated good judgment. The set of such experiences thus becomes the underpinning of a skill.

Finally, one moment was more crucial than any other during her first iteration, and that's when she invoked all skills simultaneously. The moment when the Director of System Design made the side comment about larger systems came right at the point when everything seemed lost for our innovator. But because she had learned enough on the ground level; because she had abstracted sufficiently to hold multiple and even conflicting truths about her innovative idea in her head; and because she was not intimidated by going in a completely different direction, she could create an opening within the span of minutes, turn the conversation around and enter a vast new space of possibilities. Most fundamental and medium-scale innovations encounter such turning-point moments, often more than once.

Teams and Environments

Some combination of our innovator's skills is necessary for executing any iterative innovation process. For incremental innovations — which improve a product or process, but neither require nor cause substantial changes in how things are done — the scope of required learning and abstraction is reduced and there is less need for coping with uncertainty. However, fundamental and medium-scale innovations place high demands on innovators across the spectrum of their capabilities and across the areas of Technology, Market and Implementation as well. Since individuals who have all the abilities required and can operate in all of the areas are relatively rare, can we not perform the iterative innovation process better in a group, where not everybody has to be able to do and know everything? The process inevitably involves more than one person anyway.

Let us consider then a group of individuals with talent concentrated in each of the three areas of Technology, Market and Implementation, but with the ability to understand somewhat the other areas. They can innovate as a group because they are able to communicate and iterate *together*. Teams composed of individuals with strict experiences in only one domain will fail. Such an undesirable team would consist of a person who mostly understands markets from a business perspective, such as a pure entrepreneur, a technical person who only understands technological benefits, such as a pure inventor, and an operations person who knows numbers and processes only. Although we have assembled the correct team from a high-level perspective, successful and productive iteration is not possible as the individuals do not have sufficient overlap to communicate effectively within a common reality framework. It is easy to see how such a team would have failed in face of the critical Market shift that occurred in our example.

This explains why many of the canned 1990s-version start-ups had such a low success rate for real innovation (as distinct from M&A or IPO activity, which is not a measure of real innovation delivered to the marketplace). Teams were typically assembled as stated above, and investors by default expected that there would be no iteration. Even though most investors could see the symptoms of iterative innovation in the form of multiple business plans as the company progressed, their financing window was largely incompatible with the long iterative process required for the more fundamental forms of innovation, with repeated iteration across Technology, Market and Implementation — for which their start-up teams were ill equipped in the first place.

Therefore such investors were really looking for an investment after all risk in each category had been removed. For such investors, the ideal is that a product is selected for a market, and management executes. An investor practicing this formula soon realizes that this model can only work after most of the innovation process has occurred, and only very incremental innovation is required. If a great degree of uncertainty has been removed, then such a team selection may bear fruit since most of the innovation process is complete. Of course, this is the riddle of early stage investing: in such a case, the investment is really late and not as risky as perceived, and returns are lower as the innovation is easily recognized by a large part of the investing market. Beginning in the early part of the first decade of this century, most early stage investors encountered this reality, and the bulk of such funds moved farther down in the pipeline, essentially becoming low-risk capital at high-risk capital costs.

Bottom line: investors should avoid entrepreneur-inventor-operations trios composed of non-interdisciplinary individuals at all costs. Conversely, an ideal early investing scenario with a potential for high return would be an interdisciplinary team of members who have proven they can understand all three domains of Market, Technology and Implementation, jointly as a group rather than as individuals covering each domain separately. This alleviates the burden on a single innovator to have to cover everything and introduces the additional benefit of constructive critical discussions. However, the ability to constantly learn from each other to move forward in synch, and the ability to communicate across boundaries within a common reality framework at all times, requires great teamwork skills and a lack of selfish behavior and interests. Even in such a team setting, it remains true that multidisciplinary innovators with technical backgrounds, but also with experience in Market and Implementation are desired. The team can accommodate somewhat less all-roundedness in each person as compared to the individual innovator, but all the essential innovation skill must still exist in each and every one. Of course, the identification of such a potentially successful innovation team, and productive interaction with them on a continued basis, requires the investors to be interdisciplinary themselves. People who are not interdisciplinary have a need to classify people into stereotypes in order to feel comfortable with the process.

The ideal time for investing, based on the typical 10+ year delay for fundamental innovations to reach the marketplace, would be after such an innovation team has been working on their innovative idea together for approximately five years. Examples of bad innovation investing arise from immediately creating a company based on a scientific breakthrough at a university.

This brings us to the organizational difficulty of the iterative innovation process. Even if interdisciplinary individuals make up the team, in what organizations can they iterate? A university may be creating new scientific knowledge and useful pieces of Technology, but, in general, information about the relevant Market needs and knowledge of Implementation does not exist. Corporations have segments of particular Markets understood, but typically have no insight into other markets, and they have a very short Technology horizon today. Parts of the government are like the university or like the corporation, or like neither. The Department of Defense is unusual in that it acts both like a corporate customer of innovation and like an investor in technologies in order to acquire those technologies externally in the future. Typically, however, government sectors possess little experience in all three areas of Technology, Market and Implementation. New and small enterprises seem like the best organizations to handle the innovation process, in many senses, but their downsides already have been mentioned. They may lack sufficient resources or Market access for many innovations, and we have seen over the past two decades how start-ups became severely distorted by the investing process and the need for short-term horizons due to cash flow requirements.

The difficulties in having the iterative innovation process occur in individuals, teams, and organizations should blatantly reveal how meta-stable and sensitive the process is, and how easily it is impacted by macroeconomic and organizational changes. We will develop this theme much further in the chapters ahead. In Chapter 5, as we get into the true story of a fundamental innovation evolving over a sustained period, you will see how tricky it can be to actually "sustain" the process within a series of shifting and frequently sub-optimal environments. From there we'll move into direct examination of the crumbling support system for innovation in the U.S., and how it could be rebuilt.

Meanwhile, the chapter coming up right now is a brief stage-setter for all of this.

Chapter 4

Characteristics of Fundamental Innovation

This chapter is devoted to clearing up some basic questions about innovation, such as: How big is big? What's fundamental about "fundamental"? Who does what? And the perennial favorite of so many people, when do we get the money?

It is especially important to understand "fundamental" innovation, both in the sense of defining the term and in the sense of grasping what it entails in reality. A good place to start is with what constitutes an innovation in the first place. In the eyes of some, if we are to be discussing and thinking about innovations, then in order to be included in the discussion, a creative act or product would have to be something fairly "big". That is, it would have to impact a fairly large number of people or be worth a substantial amount, or something of that order. (The very notion of "big" is not always clear.) But surely, for instance, Google or anti-lock braking systems would qualify as innovations, whereas by this line of thinking, our restaurant owner rearranging tables and chairs in her rural restaurant probably would not.

We disagree. The definition of innovation used in this book is independent of fuzzy concepts of "size", or subjective judgments thereof. The restaurant owner's table rearrangement embodied a useful idea in the marketplace and produced revenue; therefore it is an innovation. However, there are certainly specific senses in which some innovations are of greater magnitude than others, and have greater implications than others, and we do want to make those distinctions because they are very useful.

For this, we can use the standard terms "incremental" and "fundamental" innovation — but with a couple of caveats. First, as we think about these terms, let's keep remembering not to be misled by easy or fuzzy notions of big-ness. The latest new model of the hottest car on the market may be just an incremental innovation full of other incremental innovations, whereas many fundamental innovations are invisible to us: they have to do with things like the materials that crucial parts inside a product are made of, or an arcane manufacturing technique that has made it possible to produce the product at all.

Second, rather than thinking of incremental and fundamental as hard-and-fast categories, we ask you think of them as the two ends of a continuum. At one end are the most incremental innovations; at the other end are the most fundamental, and many would rightly be placed somewhere in between. (Indeed, in this book we have spoken of "medium-scale" innovations. They either have some but not all of the characteristics of a fundamental innovation, or they have the characteristics to a lesser degree. This is simply the way innovation is, and it must be recognized.)

Now for the formal definitions. Incremental innovations are often thought of as making slight or gradual improvements to things that already exist, but without changing their nature much or changing how you have to make or use those things — and that's fairly close to the mark. To state it rigorously in the terms of this book: *Incremental innovations are the innovations that need very little iteration between Technology, Market, and Implementation.* The small amount of iteration needed may be a result of two of the areas being fixed. An example of such incremental innovation would be the early progression from one microprocessor product to the next, e.g., from the Intel x286 to the x386, and so on. After the microprocessor paradigm had already been set in motion by a more fundamental innovation previously, it was followed for decades by incremental innovation. The microprocessor market was fixed, and the business model, supply chain, etc. were mostly fixed as well.

Fundamental innovations are those that either create a new business or fundamentally extend an existing one in a way that would otherwise not be possible — that part should sound familiar so far — *and for which the full iteration between Technology, Market and Implementation needs to occur multiple times, to converge on a truly novel innovation.* The start of the microprocessor paradigm was an example. Various Markets had to be evaluated for an array of possible microprocessor technologies, and the exact Implementation was also unknown. In fact, the micro-computer was not even considered as a potential application during the initial iteration; it appeared only as iteration progressed. Thus, uncertainty in all three areas existed, and multiple iterations over time were required to converge on what we know today as the microprocessor market for personal computers.

We note that our definitions of incremental and fundamental innovation are consistent with Clayton Christensen's definitions of sustainable (incremental) and disruptive (fundamental) technology in *The Innovator's Dilemma*. However, it is important to keep in mind that we have a continuous innovation space between these endpoints, and that the degree to which uncertainty is inherent to the initial innovation process in each of Technology, Market, and Implementation determines the "magnitude" of the innovation in our definition.

The Time-to-Market Delay

Because of the difference in iterations needed, there is a clear lead-time difference between fundamental and incremental innovations in reaching the marketplace. Fundamental innovations have longer time horizons because they require more iteration between Technology, Market, and Implementation. How much longer? We've already mentioned a few times that fundamental innovations typically take 10 to 15 years to come to market *at the earliest* and now we will substantiate that. For the last several decades, we have been living, overall, in the information-age paradigm (which, as noted earlier in the book, has been driven by the Moore's Law paradigm). This paradigm gives us an excellent test bed for looking at various fundamental innovations, to see how long it takes them to reach commercial product.

For Figure 2, we have chosen four fundamental innovations of the information age. The transistor and the integrated circuit should need no explaining; the Ethernet technology is used for networking computers; and strained silicon is a materials technology that fundamentally extends the processing performance of chips — it's the innovation we will hear about in the next chapter. For each of these, we have plotted the year of the "Aha moment" in the laboratory versus the year of first significant commercial release. The "Aha moment" is defined here as the time when a prototype or demonstration proves to a small group

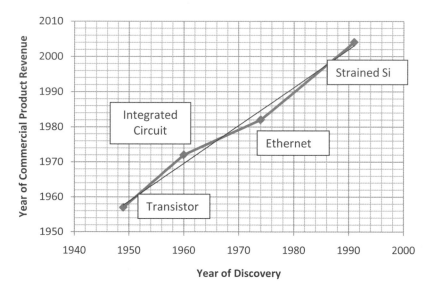

Figure 2: Approximate year of discovery vs. approximate year of significant commercial product revenue for fundamental innovations in the information age paradigm. The faired-in line indicates that fundamental innovations require 10+ years to enter the marketplace, and is fairly consistent over a wide range of different innovations.

of experts that the innovation can move beyond the laboratory; that the major beneficial features required for innovation have been demonstrated. (And please note that a good deal of work is typically required *beforehand,* just to get to that point — often, itself, involving multiple cycles of iteration!) The year of the "Aha moment" is plotted on the horizontal axis, while the vertical axis corresponds to the approximate year in which the innovation was first sold in the marketplace. Despite the common perception, these events cannot always be isolated to a particular group or person at a single occasion, so the points are meant to represent a locus of activity defining "approximately" when the events occurred. The nearly straight line connecting the points on the graph shows that a time lag of 10 years or more is pretty consistent. The information age paradigm supplies the best data for establishing this inherent time delay for fundamental innovation, because it represents the market sector dominated by free-market dynamics with the most significant growth over the past half-century.

Such data confirms the uncomfortable and often ignored messiness of the innovation process. Commercialized fundamental technology does not move very quickly to the marketplace, but is developed, tried, and evolved over lengthy periods of time. The effect of "the winners write history" is typically at play, leaving the impression that the path to commercial return is much shorter than it actually is. The 10-to-15 year delay also defines the *minimum* time needed for a fundamental innovation to *deliver its value* to the marketplace. Significant impact isn't always seen right after commercial release, either, as the innovation may take time to penetrate markets and be adopted, being iterated even further in that process: it doesn't always sweep through dramatically, changing the world in a flash. Finally, fundamental innovation could take much longer than 10 or 15 years to arrive. Our data has "survivorship bias", i.e., we have selected a few known successful fundamental innovations. A much larger number encounter snags or long lapses during which they linger on the shelf, and may take many more years to reach market, or never reach it.

Therefore, to judge what new benefits the current innovation pipeline could possibly deliver to us tomorrow or sometime soon, we need to look backwards a decade or so, to see what might be coming. The picture we get here is quite different from the common perception that once a working embodiment of an invention is made in a lab, its potential has been "proved" in such a manner that surely, the economic rewards can't be far behind. A realistic grasp of the timelines between fundamental invention and high commercial return is needed in order to understand anything about our innovation system.

Note that the innovations in Fig. 2 are very different in nature: a device, a complex system in miniature, a network, and a material. This implies that the 10 to 15 year delay between "Aha moment" and first commercial dollar earned for fundamental innovations is inherent under free market conditions, and does not depend on the type of technology. That observation should raise serious questions about the calls for "accelerating the innovation process" that we so often hear. By optimizing the support for iterative innovation throughout the innovation ecosystem, we can try to make sure that no *additional* delays are introduced, or that potential innovations are not driven to premature failure by forces outside the innovation process. But reducing the inherent 10 to 15 year *minimum* delay from "Aha" to commercial release is unfortunately not feasible in the case of fundamental innovations.

A clear way to see why this is so, beyond acknowledging the data, is to think about what has to happen in the real world and how it contributes to this delay. There are essentially two ways in which a fundamental innovation can be physically implemented. Either one has to create an entirely new industry supply chain because there is none to begin with, as Apple had to do for the microcomputer in the 1970s, or one has to insert the fundamental innovation into a fairly mature supply chain. Of course variations can be found on the spectrum between these two extremes — you might need to create some parts of your supply chain, while also making use of what exists — but either involves a lot of work. Creating a new supply chain requires many new suppliers, which in turn requires thousands of people doing things they have not done before. The participants in the new supply chain need to be educated and motivated, and their organizations need to be rewarded. Also, different participants must be able to iterate across Market, Technology, and Implementation together to define their respective relationships. The mobilization of such a force takes time, and is ultimately limited by teaching people to do new things. And now let's consider the other option. To inject a fundamental innovation into the middle of a mature supply chain, the innovators must work to get those below them to supply into their new level, and those above them must learn how to incorporate the innovation and learn why it is beneficial to them. The requirement of further iteration together is also true for this case, while most of the time and effort will be spent on changing existing behaviors. In both cases, we can think of this delay as originating from the limitations of human learning, communication, and mobilization. Ultimately, the 10-to-15 year delay is required for people and organizations to adapt to a fundamental shift.

People and Roles

Beyond the relation between invention and innovation discussed thus far, let us define "inventor", "innovator", and "entrepreneur" for clarity. An inventor is someone who creates a technology — a widget, or a process — which could be valuable based on its novel functionality. However, the invention has generally not been run through the iterative innovation process, which is the only way of determining its value. The inventor may turn into an innovator by interacting with the marketplace, employing additional other technologies in order to make a viable product, and also modifying the invention due to implementation realities. Typically, the innovation process enables more purposeful subsequent "inventing" activity, as consecutive iterations provide more and more resolution on useful embodiments. At any rate, an innovator works in all three areas of Technology, Market and Implementation in order to converge on an innovation, which is the commercially viable form of the invention.

As for the entrepreneur: strictly speaking, the entrepreneur's role is that of starting and growing a new venture, and this person is primarily concerned with the business mechanics of doing so. Our society has created the model of an individual who does it all, inventing, innovating, and growing the business, but this is not necessarily the case nor is it the ideal. Innovators enable new-company formation and growth, while entrepreneurs execute on growing the business, which they cannot do unless a viable innovation is in place. They should thus enter, ideally, when the innovation process has already largely converged.

The distinction of inventor, innovator, and entrepreneur is important in discussing and understanding the innovation process. The case of an entrepreneur being inventor and innovator as well is rare, but the success of some of these individuals has amplified the perception that this is the norm. Thomas Edison was an example of an inventor, innovator, and entrepreneur. He played all roles in developing products and services in the emerging electrical industry. His contemporary Nikola Tesla also played a vital part, but mainly as a prolific inventor, and while Tesla is a virtual cult hero in many high-tech circles he is much less known among the general public: thus the distinction gets lost.

The Ecosystem

Although the highest return occurs for fundamental innovation, we want to emphasize that the entire spectrum between fundamental and incremental innovations is required for a healthy innovation ecosystem. Viewed one by one, incremental innovations may seem to be of "minor" consequence but they are important for many reasons. Their value adds up, both collectively and over time. Even on the individual scale, just a small improvement can sometimes make a big difference to a person using or selling a product, and so forth. Innovations closer to the incremental end of the scale are also more easily made and supported. They are easily financed and evaluated by traditional financial metrics. Therefore that section of the innovation pipeline — the set of systems for supporting incremental innovation — does not change appreciably over time.

Fundamental innovations are much more sensitive to the state of the innovation ecosystem and pipeline, and past changes to these affect the viability of our innovation processes and our economy in the present. It is also the fundamental innovations that produce sustainable economic growth over longer periods. We may think that recent economic times have been difficult enough, but if the semiconductor and microcomputer revolutions had not occurred, from their innovative beginnings in places like the Boston area and the Bay Area, what would the many millions who now work in the related industries be doing? What would be the state of the American economy; the global economy?

Incremental innovation will be preserved over time, since the more narrow skill set and short timescale for financing are more easily met by society. But it is fundamental innovation that has defined the industrial and information ages, and that must create the paradigms for our future growth and prosperity. Not only do we need to support the nature of the iterative innovation process for fundamental innovation, but we need to be mindful of how the critical time-delay factor plays into the past, present and future of our innovation ecosystem, so that investors, innovators, inventors, politicians, etc. can all realistically plan and execute on their own visions for optimizing innovation.

The next chapter gives us a ground-level view of a fundamental innovation as it unfolded over a 20-year period.

Chapter 5

The Story of a Fundamental Innovation

We are going to take you on an exceptional real-life journey. It is the story of a fundamental innovation that you are probably making use of, and benefiting from, every day, although you probably aren't aware of it. You will see the end-to-end innovation process through the eyes of the primary innovator. At the close of the chapter are three much briefer stories of other innovations, which round out the picture by showing how the process can go forward in somewhat different ways.

All stories are about innovations that we, the authors, have been involved with. We have taken part in numerous fundamental or medium-scale innovation processes over the years. The activities have been performed in corporations, in universities, and in start-up companies. Two of us, Gene Fitzgerald and Andreas Wankerl, also have started a nonprofit entity called Innovation Interface for collaborative projects between universities and corporations, and that has helped deepen our knowledge as well.

The main story in the chapter is Gene Fitzgerald's. He lived it intimately from start to finish for nearly 20 years, as the primary innovator, and that alone makes the story valuable. Many written accounts of modern-day innovations pick up the process somewhere in midstream, with perhaps only a summary of the work that went before. It is hard then to get a grasp of how truly "messy" the process can be, how repeated iterations are needed to resolve uncertainties from the very beginning, and how what was decided in early stages influences what is done later. This story traces out the five years of basic research and initial iterating that it took to arrive at what the innovation actually *is* — and then follows the process through 14 more years en route to the form in which you have the innovation today.

What also makes the story unique and valuable is that it took place across multiple environments over a time when the U.S. innovation system, the country's pipeline for innovation, was evolving and being altered into the present structure that is now, itself, deteriorating rapidly. So you will get first-hand views of an innovation system in transition and how the system affects the process of innovating.

The fundamental innovation that is the subject of the story is "strained silicon electronics". It is a technology for making integrated circuits, which can greatly enhance their performance. Very likely you have strained silicon in your computer chips. The technological details of strained silicon are very complex and are kept to a minimum here. Simply keep in mind that when a layer of silicon is "strained" in just the right manner — either pulled at the edges, or squeezed together compressively — its properties change, and the integrated circuits etched into the material can be made to perform vastly better.

In what follows we're going to shift between Gene telling his own story in the first person and occasional pull-backs to reflect and comment. To keep the distinction clear, all of the first-person narrative is indented.

Gene Fitzgerald's Story: Strained Silicon Electronics

If we were to go back to the earliest origins of this innovation, the story would have to start in my childhood. I was always driven to build technological widgets, being one of those children who grow up with potent chemistry and electronics sets in the basement. The desire to actually build something rather than just experiment with nature was probably significant, because it surfaced when I was in graduate school in materials science at Cornell University in the late 1980s. In surveying different research groups to decide on a PhD research topic, I was puzzled to notice that much research, although scientifically interesting, appeared not to be connected to anything directly useful. To me, conducting research in that way seemed a bit arbitrary and random. Fortunately I found a PhD advisor, Dieter Ast, who regularly spent time at Hewlett-Packard's basic research laboratories in Palo Alto during the summers. After a couple of conversations, it seemed he had an interesting project related to the materials for making high speed integrated circuits — the kind that are important for advanced electronics in measurement and telecommunications. The project involved characterizing a material called gallium arsenide, which many had assumed would eventually replace the dominant material used in integrated circuits, silicon. Generally speaking, any such material needs to be very close to perfect on an atomic scale to be useful for advanced electronic or optical applications.

I built, by hand, special characterization equipment to be able to look at the material microscopically in a way that would reveal some unknowns about its imperfections. Although I had a thrill of success in demonstrating that the equipment worked, it seemed my characterization of gallium arsenide was losing relevance in the outside industrial research world; it wasn't clear that it would have significant use. But now another fortunate contact helped: Jerry Woodall. A Cornell graduate and IBM Fellow (and today a National Medal of Technology Laureate), he was actively involved on campus. This dynamic corporate researcher was a classic "loose gun" within the IBM research lab, where the purpose of the Fellows program was to allow such individuals to "do their own thing" based on track records of previous invention and innovation. Jerry explained to me his thoughts about how new electronics built in gallium arsenide would evolve. He felt that new materials *related* to gallium arsenide could be deposited on gallium arsenide, making them even better, but there were some fundamental materials problems that blocked progress along that route. A graduate-student colleague had introduced me to Jerry because she realized I could look at some of the problems with my new characterization tool. Jerry agreed to use his resources at IBM to make a set of materials samples for me to examine.

Indeed, I could see defects at the interfaces between materials. After some work, it dawned on me that there might be a way to prevent these defects from entering. That would allow an electronic device application that

Jerry had mentioned to possibly work in the future. I teamed up with another graduate student at the central facilities on campus to fabricate a new set of materials, to see if my idea would in fact prevent the defects. It did. This was a very striking result. Within the specialized field of electronic materials, I had now made a name for myself even as a graduate student and the success allowed me to graduate early. My search for job opportunities was focused on the industrial basic research laboratories such as IBM's Watson Research Center, AT&T Bell Labs, HP Labs and others. When an interviewer at AT&T Bell Labs asked if I was interested in a university position, I said "No way". It seemed clear to me that the industrial labs were the places where applications and fundamental science intersected, which meant that basic research that could lead to real innovations with real impact had a much higher chance of occurring there.

AT&T Bell Labs expressed interest in hiring me not only because of my educational background and the research results I had produced, but because of the growing importance of this research area inside the Labs. AT&T made everything from transistors to telecommunication systems, and advances in the materials I had worked with could impact a wide variety of applications. I accepted the offer.

Let's pause in the story to identify some key aspects of the very earliest stages of a fundamental innovation. First, note that the choice of PhD research area came from an interest in practical relevance. The research topic became the incipient Technology in the innovation process, a topic that had practical potential as well as scientific interest and was found through a faculty advisor connected to outside Market and Implementation knowledge. Later contacts with similar knowledge helped move the process along. As we shall see in more detail during the next part of the story, the major corporate research laboratories of the time were infused with the Market and Implementation knowledge of their industry sectors. It's been said that the cafeteria at AT&T Bell Labs was one of the most fertile places in the world for knowledge exchange, a place where a dark-matter physicist could sit down next to someone working on a communications laser for a specific use. One learns what is needed; the other learns what is possible.

At universities then it was also a common, though far from ubiquitous, practice that university experts would regularly spend significant time in industrial labs, and that industrial experts would regularly spend significant time at the university. This created an application-rich environment in which Market and Implementation knowledge shaped the choices of at least some important basic research problems at universities.

Through the building of the gallium arsenide characterization tool and its role in finding a way to prevent defects, we can see the Technology work being informed by Market information from multiple directions. That is useful, focused iteration. However, we don't see Fitzgerald devoting great effort yet to figuring out what *his* "end product" would be or what "business model" would work best. For instance, he is not forming a start-up company around selling the characterization tool or materials engineering services. It might be a possibility to be discussed, but jumping directly into it at this point would be very premature. On that note, here are two related observations:

In the basic industrial research labs of large and mature firms in the 1980s, the business model was always inherent, i.e. researchers were expected to assume their work would wind up being deployed in some existing unit or units of the company. The previous dominance of these companies seemed to imply that when something important was developed, "someone in the company" would have the optimum use for it and know how to commercialize it. Such an assumption also avoided the difficulty associated with the innovation converging on market space outside the company's current market domain. For this and other reasons, these laboratories were excellent at the early stage of fundamental innovation iteration but often poor toward the later stage, when the innovation needed to be more intimately absorbed into the marketplace.

Also note that at this point in Fitzgerald's story, there is absolutely no way to predict the emergence of strained silicon as a consequence of the innovation path. He isn't even working with silicon — yet. But we must emphasize that the inability to see a direct link between early research and the final application is not a justification for *starting at any point* in research space. Often, the unrecorded messiness of the innovation process leads supporters of "random investigative research" to conclude that since the end application cannot *exactly* be determined at the beginning, simply funding early stage research according to the random whim of researchers is sufficient. It will be clear from this recording of the actual messy innovation process that such a conclusion is invalid. The constant iteration between Market, Technology, and Implementation is required for performing excellent research, as well as for maintaining the potential to converge on a fundamental innovation. Returning to our story:

My first day at Bell Labs in the fall of 1988 was like arriving in paradise. I was starting my career at the Labs site in Murray Hill, New Jersey, where many famous discoveries occurred, including the transistor. I had my picture on a Bell Labs ID badge and had achieved a dream that began in the basement when I was in elementary school. I was ready to invent for Bell Labs, to bring important research discoveries to market.

I was moved into what was apparently a very famous office, since the previous occupant had discovered the CO_2 gas laser more than a decade earlier. A Bell Labs manager two levels above me visited to tell me this, and to advise me, "You had better be great". Next, I met with my immediate manager. After some small talk, I began expounding upon how my research direction could lead to many significant results for electronic materials and devices. This skilled manager, not wanting to crush my enthusiasm, said that all of those ideas were great, very exciting. Then he asked, "In what ways do you think your research direction can be of greatest impact to AT&T?" Well. In my work in graduate school I had thought about IBM's needs, and through other interactions with the industry-infused research community of the time, I was starting to be able to generalize Market needs for electronic and optical applications. Now I was being asked about the specific issue of AT&T's Market impact on my first day.

I started thinking, quickly, as follows. I had been hired into a department within a larger Labs organization interested in gallium arsenide and related materials. My department was to look at extending some of the layered materials advances in this area to involve silicon, the material from which most integrated circuits are built. I recalled a conversation with my advisor about HP working on the layering problem of putting gallium arsenide on silicon. If this could be done, speculation was that many new application needs could be met, since the beneficial properties of gallium arsenide and silicon are complementary in many respects. Integrated optoelectronics was the Holy Grail application, where light and electricity could both be used to make incredible super-chips useful in computers and computer networks.

I replied to my manager that when silicon scaling (i.e. Moore's Law) slows down, some 20 years into the future, being able to integrate gallium arsenide with silicon would allow silicon technology to be carried further. Since AT&T was involved in both computers and communications, my manager said, "Excellent, then that is what you should do. If that is the most important problem in this area for AT&T, and has the highest long term impact, that is what you should do".

Easier said than done. How would a new, naïve PhD start down this path? I could start research on gallium arsenide on silicon immediately, since that research would be an extension of work I was already involved in. But how would I really understand how that would impact integrated optoelectronics for AT&T? What would the layered material be incorporated into? What were the most important aspects of the materials' properties? And how would they relate to the performance of the devices that made up the circuits, which in turn became part of the systems that were to be ultimately used by the Market?

Fortunately, AT&T Bell Labs had many interfaces between research areas (Technology) and application areas (Implementation and Market). This fact is consistently neglected in reports about the original AT&T Bell Labs, while the eventual overlap with academic laboratories appears overemphasized. Asking around, I found out that a couple of researchers at the Bell Labs site in Holmdel, New Jersey were interested in this problem at the communication-system level. After contact via phone and email, the system-level researchers warmly welcomed my interest. Although researchers themselves, they acted effectively as a customer to my more basic research, because it could help them with the needs of their internal customers. This chain of virtual customer-supplier relations all the way down to the most basic research was an essential feature of Bell Labs that aided innovation. You didn't have to count on being lucky enough to sit down next to the right person in the cafeteria. Experts in areas from basic research to applications were mostly open to inquiries from other areas of AT&T. It was cultural to begin with, but had been accelerated by divestiture of AT&T's numerous local telephone companies in 1984. Within a very short time, I had found the connection between my work and a critical AT&T need. Light waves were now part of the long distance telecommunication infrastructure, and it was clear that light would be used to move information at shorter and shorter distances in the future, as both silicon integrated circuits and light-based communication systems continued to improve.

With this application in mind, I had some idea of how the layered structure might be created for an integrated circuit that could have both optical elements, such as lasers and detectors, and silicon electronics on the same chip. Through continued interaction with integrated circuit experts, my knowledge of silicon integrated circuits, in general, expanded. The gallium arsenide and related materials, in which the optical elements had to be built, needed to be joined perfectly with the silicon on an atomic scale through engineering processes overcoming their natural misfit. With some knowledge from the experiments I had done in graduate school, I saw that layering these materials would not be possible without using an intermediate material to accommodate some of the problems. This material was silicon germanium. I set out to determine how to deposit silicon germanium on silicon materials in order to ultimately make the silicon germanium surface compatible for gallium arsenide.

A stunning breakthrough occurred, allowing very high quality silicon germanium to be deposited on silicon. Although the material was not the right composition to allow the further integration of the gallium arsenide material, it was clear from the characterization data that the breakthrough should eventually be extended to make this possible. However, management was more dubious of the significance, being aware of fewer details. What management saw was progress, but this Fitzgerald guy still could not integrate gallium arsenide on silicon. In addition, the management changed. My previous manager had left AT&T, and the new manager wanted to review all activity and determine if the research focus should be shifted. I needed a real demonstration that the material was high quality; I needed another application that might benefit from the material on a shorter time scale.

Just before the silicon germanium advance, I had started working with a new colleague, Ya-Hong Xie. He had graduated from a research group at UCLA where some very early work in silicon germanium was attempted. Although no great fundamental innovations were generated in this group at the time, Ya-Hong was also thinking of how his research interest intersected with AT&T's goals. It was only a matter of time before Ya-Hong and I realized that the silicon germanium material was good enough to create a material called strained silicon.

Theoretically, it long had been predicted that a highly strained silicon layer would have very beneficial electrical properties. However, no one had solved the problem of the silicon germanium that I had just solved, and that would allow a high quality strained silicon layer to exist. Ya-Hong and I immediately set out to create the first high quality strained silicon. Within the first batch of experiments, we accomplished this goal, in 1990. Only two years after joining Bell Labs, I had an important "discovery", or as we have more appropriately defined it in this book, the start of a potential fundamental innovation. The news quickly spread worldwide, and key groups at British Telecom, Daimler-Benz, and IBM immediately recognized that the research result could have impact on silicon integrated circuits, the very technology behind the information age paradigm. Within months, Dailmer-Benz laboratories reproduced the Bell Labs result. Due to the status of these world renowned laboratories, the discovery was vetted as real and important, at least to the extent that it was the basis for a future potential innovation.

Let us pause again to connect back to iterative innovation. Iteration between Technology, Market and Implementation had occurred even before the "strained silicon" discovery. Unlike in an academic environment, Bell Labs management immediately informed Fitzgerald of his need to excel, and excel in an area important for the business of AT&T. The definition of "excellent research" included not just great science, and not just great potential for applicability, but also a subtle pressure to have that science or technology become an actual innovation for AT&T. The problem choice largely belonged to the researcher, but the Market context belonged to AT&T, and the Implementation was again assumed to be the "AT&T System". As discussed for IBM previously, it was assumed that valuable innovations would naturally be commercialized.

Finding internal "customers" for his research and learning about the realities of circuit and systems design, Fitzgerald iterated his proposed research through Market and Implementation with much more detail. This iteration resulted in the correct identification of silicon germanium as the intermediate layer material. If this iteration had not been successful, he would have had to redefine his research. The Technology breakthrough (high quality silicon germanium) enabled the next iteration with his colleague Ya-Hong Xie through Market (now also including logic chips and microprocessors) and Implementation (enhanced electronics performance through strained silicon).

Corporate structure in this story is playing an important but not always obvious role. AT&T housed an entire spectrum of researchers and engineers working in areas of importance to the company, from the very basic to the applied, but unlike in a university, this expertise was not spread across the entire world of scientific research. Because of the culture of research excellence and desire to show their skills throughout AT&T, experts in various areas gladly shared their knowledge, allowing Fitzgerald to quickly gain Market information from real transactional experiences, not just notional ones. This ability to have a very "low transaction cost" with respect to iterative innovation is not included in modern organizational economic concepts, but should be. At the same time, the high *innovation productivity* of such large bureaucratic companies has been ignored, largely due to the inefficient *absorption* of innovations in such bureaucracies. Finally, Implementation knowledge in the realms of manufacturing and complex system design was also diffused to Fitzgerald. These pieces of the picture allowed Fitzgerald and Xie to rapidly converge on significant milestones along the path of this fundamental innovation.

The excitement of the breakthrough passed after a period of time. A few extra people were added to our research effort, which allowed many more details of the fundamental invention to be revealed, and many researchers around the world started to produce results that further discerned the potential and details of the now-burgeoning field of strained silicon. I grew anxious that AT&T would not be the first to commercialize the invention. Great at the early stage of fundamental innovation, AT&T was known for missing out on the later stages. I drove the nascent group towards the ultimate objective: room temperature silicon electronics, made using processes easily translated to manufacturing, which demonstrated far superior performance. Only 27 years old and quite naïve about the resources required for continued iterative innovation through early and full-stage development, I could soon see that a group of five people and no additional resources could not create an entire new silicon integrated circuit technology, even in Bell Labs with all of the best people nearby.

By 1994, I perceived that advancing the innovation towards market application was nearly impossible in the present environment. The firm had no system for moving research to pilot production, nor did I sense much urgency about it. Since I was now so well known for the invention of high quality strained silicon, universities were contacting me. Would I still say "no way" to a faculty position? I was still unsure whether a university would have enough real contact with the world of applications to create a proper environment for continuing the work.

As AT&T faced an ever more competitive business environment, it was clear that the previous "venture model of research" had been eliminated. In the late 1980s and early 1990s, most corporations that had forward-looking research labs began to winnow their investments in basic research. In this time period at AT&T, management was also trying to quantify the actual investment return on Bell Labs. I had assumed previously that management knew how to value and commercialize research. Although our strained silicon work was a perfect example of how basic research in the environment at AT&T could produce fundamental innovation, these management reviews over the years made me realize that no one really knew how to move embryonic fundamental innovations closer to the marketplace. I asked myself, "How can Bell Labs survive without a purpose?" My interest in the interdisciplinary space between research and commercialization was ignited, out of frustration and now, intellectual curiosity.

Since most corporate basic research labs were encountering similar pressures and therefore found themselves in the process of being eliminated in the early 1990s, I hoped that there might be one-stop-shopping in the future at key research universities. Who, other than young innovators from these top institutions, could become the future source of innovation? In the fall of 1994, I returned to my undergraduate alma mater, MIT, as a faculty member. I wanted to work with young people who could be trained as innovators, and to further develop an understanding about fundamental technology commercialization.

Upon arrival at MIT, the full extent of the risk I had taken was upon my shoulders. A month after moving to the university my wife gave birth to twins. Our cash flow was reduced compared to my previous corporate salary. In addition, I did not have tenure, and my initial start-up funds for a research group were less than half of what my AT&T research start-up funds had been. Finally, some equipment I had thought I could acquire for free now looked like it might not find its way to MIT, and the lab space that had been promised to me was pre-empted by internal politics. It was clear that the strained silicon field, which I and Ya-Hong had been so fortunate to start, might now leave me behind. However, I had come here with the idea that I was testing MIT to see whether it could be the right environment for me, and if not, I had some vague notion of starting my own venture someday in the Boston area. Besides, from a social perspective, my wife and I were now closer to our family support structures as we both had been raised in communities outside Boston.

This section marks the first organizational transition made to allow the iterative innovation process to continue. Fitzgerald directly experienced the inability of a large company to absorb and continue successful early-stage fundamental innovation, when the company becomes at the same time more driven by competitive pressures and more sclerotic internally. Bureaucratic inflation on the operational side had disaggregated Implementation knowledge, and precluded getting the broader Market knowledge necessary for completing iterative innovation. Even in an organization that was optimized for high fundamental innovation productivity, such as Bell Labs within AT&T, the financial and organizational structure of AT&T would prevent further iterative innovation.

If the innovator cannot move the organization, then the innovator must move the innovation to another organization. The importance of organizational mobility is now clear. So far, tracking it from the start, the evolution of a fundamental innovation has required Fitzgerald to work with highly mobile university and corporate researchers at Cornell University, then prompted him to move from academe to AT&T Bell Labs, and now brought him to MIT. Around the time of this latest move, in the early 1990s, other innovators at prominent U.S. industrial research laboratories had been experiencing equivalent problems and taking similar steps. Moving to universities along with their partially completed innovations, many became prime candidates for venture capital investment. Here were smart people with innovations that had been vetted for business potential by major firms. Those innovations often had been carried to a point that embodied the value of substantial past investment. A smart investor could now succeed by capturing the value of work already paid for, funding it the rest of the way and bringing it to the marketplace.

Potential innovators must, on average, follow the innovation as opposed to following the organization if there is to be a high rate of innovation. The innovator moves to gain the freedom for, and to seek resources for, continuing the iterative process. As in this story, such a move is typically accompanied by an increase in personal risk and a decrease in resources to continue the innovation (absent a shower of exuberant venture capital). These disadvantages must be outweighed by the innovator's confidence in the innovation and his or her abilities, which can act as a useful quality filter as long as the innovation ecosystem generally supports such mobility. Any system in which mobility is lowered by imposing too many disadvantages on the innovator, financially or culturally, will clearly decrease the rate of fundamental innovation.

Here I was at MIT, struggling to put a research infrastructure in place. This included recruiting graduate students. With little to show to those wishing to step into an established research group, I attracted an initial set of PhD candidates interested in building real things and performing research that has some connection to real applications. In other words, I was now attracting a sub-set of students who were using the same criterion for their advisor choice as I had done. This helped greatly, in part because the first real things that had to be built were the lab and the research group itself. Within two years, the Fitzgerald Group at MIT was back at the cutting edge in strained silicon, and started making progress on some of the new research problems which had been exposed by the earlier work. In other places, the growing research community that had been sparked by our initial work at Bell Labs was decaying and moving on to other pursuits since early advances in the area were complete. Also, large basic corporate R&D labs were closing up shop, eliminating continued work in this area. However, our lab continued to pursue the innovation. At the time of my transition to MIT, the strained silicon material was of high enough quality that single electronic elements with enhanced performance could be demonstrated in the laboratory — if one fabricated them on just the right patch of material. A market application would require integrated circuits without defects over much larger areas, capable of being mass-produced at high yield with the type of production technology in which the information age had already invested billions of dollars.

My knowledge of this production technology with all its parameters, which I had learned from many interactions with the production implementation folks at AT&T and other companies, led to the identification of two fundamental research problems blocking the innovation path for strained silicon. One was related to infrequent defects that most researchers ignored, because one could circumvent them for single laboratory demonstration devices, but they were very important on the scale of actual electronic circuits. The other was a problem related to maintaining long range surface flatness, due to the inherent strains in the material, which again could be ignored for individual electronic elements in the lab but not for making actual circuits. Both were fundamental research problems that produced leading edge science, *and* removed barriers to potential future commercialization. While most academic researchers and funding agencies turned their backs on these problems at the time, our group and very few others around the world stayed on the strained silicon innovation path. Our group ultimately produced the second big scientific breakthrough in the field. Although achieved while working on strained silicon, this breakthrough turned out to be equally important for the possible alternative innovation of integrating gallium arsenide and related materials.

Briefly interrupting the story again, we note that another iteration of the innovation process has occurred. Identifying the right Technology research to work on at MIT was the result of iterating yet another time through Market and Implementation. The Market valuation required strained silicon electronics to be competitive with conventional silicon electronics. This imposed the requirement on the Implementation side that strained silicon electronics must be manufactured by using the existing industry infrastructure with a comparable production yield. This, in turn, defined the Technology problems that had to be overcome by fundamental research, leading to the scientific breakthroughs. Interestingly, these breakthroughs were as important for the other potential applications, because achieving silicon-type production economics would result in significant cost advantages for the other potential Markets.

Around the time of the second Technology breakthrough, I sensed that "really good Bell Labs research", i.e. the kind that is fundamental but guided by real Market needs and Implementation possibilities, would soon be finished in strained silicon, at least from a university perspective. Clearly I could have spent the rest of my life in academe studying the nuances of a research area I had originated. However, I sensed that there was nothing else fundamental to do at the university level, and that the group at MIT should move on to related topics like advancing device performance through strained germanium instead of strained silicon. Strained silicon now needed another transition; I felt that all of the remaining challenges could only be really worked on in a more commercial environment with direct Market and Implementation exposure. Although I wasn't quite sure of tenure, nor of how strained silicon could evolve outside the university, I laid the groundwork by forming a company called AmberWave Technologies in 1996. Bringing it into official existence entailed filling out a one-page form and paying about $100 to the State of New Hampshire. (The company later became AmberWave Systems Corporation).

But in order to engage in any kind of interaction with an interested outside party, AmberWave needed some capability to fabricate prototypes and develop them further. I could use a central facility at MIT for that, but now I needed to know more about the interface of the university to the outside world. What was considered a conflict of interest? How was it possible to even move technology from campus? How could a university entrepreneur survive, instantaneously going from a resourced environment to one of zero resources? All of the "special sauce" involved in making strained silicon prototypes required the use of a range of expensive equipment that was only available at central university facilities or in sizable production companies. All ideas would be stillborn with no outside resources in the game.

In my pursuit to move things along, I met with Leta Nelson, the head of MIT's Technology License Office (TLO). Leta had become TLO head following the implementation of the Bayh-Dole Act of 1980, which allowed universities to hold intellectual property for research carried out under government-funded programs. She explained the main conflicts of interest. The ones I needed to avoid at this stage were pretty straightforward: I could not compel students, using my position as a professor, to produce anything for my external company, and could not use MIT facilities for production. However, an important aspect of technology transfer is that a small company can use a university central facility on a pay-for-use basis and for demonstration quantities. In other words, there are mechanisms in place to move technology as long as the volumes are still at research levels. In addition to explaining all of this, Leta asked me a critical question: "How will you form a new semiconductor company?"

I was stumped by the question. A silicon electronics manufacturing facility of economic scale required a capital investment of more than a billion dollars at the time. From interaction with the industry, I had been taught that modern "semiconductor companies" were actually circuit design houses that neither produced their own material nor fabricated the material into integrated circuits. Unlike the world of AT&T and other vertically integrated companies, the semiconductor world was already experiencing rapid horizontal specialization. Materials manufacturers just made silicon wafers, which the Taiwanese "silicon foundries" converted into circuits, made to specifications from the design firms that we in the U.S. still grandly called semiconductor companies. Only the large microprocessor companies, such as Intel and

Advanced Micro Devices (AMD), still fabricated some of their own circuits, but didn't make their own material either. Given that supply chain, Leta was therefore essentially asking what business model I was going to pursue. The only new start-up companies at the time were just design houses. I had a materials innovation, and going into the microprocessor market, if only to serve big companies like Intel or AMD as a materials supplier, would require huge production volumes.

Optimistically I figured there must be a way to transfer value into the marketplace. Maybe such a large industry was not the place to enter. I wondered if there were smaller-volume industries or special niches where AmberWave could start by producing material and then grow vertically over time, eventually producing circuits. Although this seemed logical, the high degree of specialization that was previously required by large corporations seemed to create a culture of territory, and convention dictated that materials innovators do not found integrated circuit companies. I sensed already that the business model paradox would play a central part in the innovation process if the commercialization of strained silicon integrated circuits were to become a reality.

Pausing for another moment, we log the next organizational transition. Fitzgerald's move to follow the innovation was again accompanied by a loss of resources, down to zero this time. Although the personal risk remained the same at the point of incorporating AmberWave on paper, we shall see that this will change once the company is operating and cash flows become tight. The formation of Amberwave became necessary as real transactional experience with suppliers, partners, and customers was needed to further the innovation. If Fitzgerald had not formed a company capable of interacting directly in the marketplace, the technical research path undoubtedly would have varied, probably moving in a direction with a lower probability of producing a successful innovation.

Being now a practical innovator and early-stage entrepreneur, I started thinking about potential customers that would actually perform a transaction with AmberWave. The list was narrowed to three kinds of prospects. The one specific prospect at this point was Draper Laboratory, a large nonprofit lab spun out from MIT years ago, best known for its long-running work in developing navigation and tracking systems for the Department of Defense and NASA. The two further entries were "other government customers", and high-efficiency solar cell companies. That's right, I had already written off the large silicon integrated circuit industry because of the barriers to entry. The trend in that industry suggested that a new business model would not be welcomed, and the obstacles to get any initial business under way were too high. Faced with the practical need of engaging customers, AmberWave had to open up to other applications which would be enabled by the same fundamental innovation thus far achieved at AT&T Bell Labs and MIT. Other than strained silicon integrated circuits for faster microprocessors, there could be simpler but high-speed electronics in silicon germanium (the intermediate layer material) for wireless communications, or devices in gallium arsenide and related materials on silicon (the original materials technology goal at Bell Labs), for which high-efficiency solar cells would be simpler than the "Holy Grail" AT&T goal of integrated optoelectronic circuits for telecommunications. Each of these completely different applications still had its own set of technical hurdles to be overcome, but they would all fundamentally be enabled by the previous Technology breakthroughs.

Draper Laboratory was interested in silicon germanium for yet another application: electromechanical devices which integrate electronic and moving parts on a chip (such as used for triggering the airbag in a car, for example). I supplied silicon germanium samples, but it appeared that an application in electromechanical systems was speculative. Some early results seemed to indicate an unanticipated loss of performance with the material. Leaving electromechanical devices behind and looking at other government markets, Professor Steve Ringel and I had demonstrated through a university program that high efficiency thin solar films could be deposited and fabricated on silicon substrates using the same silicon-germanium layered material technology. Steve knew the government market for solar cells for satellites and spacecraft well, so AmberWave applied for Small Business Innovation Research (SBIR) contracts through NASA to fabricate the solar cells on silicon. The ability to fabricate them on silicon, and the potential of using the high-throughput silicon manufacturing infrastructure, would make the cells far less expensive than the current high efficiency cells used for these high-end applications. In addition, the silicon substrate would allow for lighter and stronger solar cells, important in space missions.

The first SBIR application failed, but with more effort to meet the customers at NASA, AmberWave submitted a new proposal. While it was in the review process in 1996–97, with three months or more between submission and award, and another few months before funds would reach a company, I was contacted by a research group leader at Motorola in Austin, Texas, where the firm manufactured its microprocessors. Apparently Motorola was interested in both the silicon germanium layered technology and the strained silicon technology that I had demonstrated at AT&T Bell Labs. Motorola was conducting early research investigations into the potential of these technologies for its chips. I was excited. This was a good lead and a visit to Motorola was arranged. But on the plane to Texas I was still debating exactly what business model to propose. What would they want? Consulting, engineering services, or would they simply buy material? I had been running some calculations on selling material, and several aspects of that business model bothered me. First, being at the lowest point in the supply chain, pure materials companies in the semiconductor industry had difficulty retaining a sufficient margin, because of the bargaining power of the circuit manufacturers. Second, a small company would need a lot of capital investment to make enough material to supply even one of Motorola's fabrication facilities. That in itself was not necessarily a problem, I thought, especially since the capital markets in 1997 were eager to invest in technology companies. But the industry was so large that gaining a sufficient margin in a high volume material supply business, after taking into account the cost of capital, would be very difficult.

I met with the group leader at Motorola, who not only was a Bell Labs alumnus, but also once had been an assistant professor in my department at MIT. With common background, we soon were having a constructive conversation on Motorola's current interest, what it could evolve to if successful, and what I could do. Taking a chance, I mentioned that I had formed AmberWave to commercialize the technology, and that Motorola should work with the company, as opposed to just having me consult. I pointed out that improvements to the technology had been made at MIT, and said AmberWave could work to expose Motorola to the best silicon germanium and strained silicon technologies that existed, long before any other corporation would be exposed. The group leader was interested, and probed further into how I saw AmberWave evolving. I told him openly that it could be a materials supply business, but that I would prefer to see AmberWave eventually producing integrated circuits on strained silicon, because the real value of the innovation could only be captured there. Calculations showed that using strained silicon for integrated electronics would translate to a performance improvement equivalent to an entire generation of silicon technology, for which each company needed to invest approximately $1 billion for each manufacturing facility at the time. The Motorola group leader encouraged me to think about the materials supply business, which he thought was a "very excellent business" for AmberWave.

I was impressed overall with the Motorola connection, although the business model question bothered me, especially the fact that Motorola seemed intent so early on boxing AmberWave into the low-margin materials supply business. I was also thinking that the breakthrough research results at MIT, which solved most of the Technology problems associated with mass-production Implementation, were fresh patent applications, and I did not want to share this information with Motorola at this point. Traveling back from Texas, I realized that intellectual property was at least one arrow in AmberWave's quiver that could be used to protect the inventions. As I kept all of this in mind through follow-up talks, we arrived at an agreement between Motorola and AmberWave within a few weeks. At this stage of the interaction the model would be one of engineering services and materials supply. The contract called for AmberWave to supply silicon germanium material of "Bell Labs quality", i.e. without the improvements that my group at MIT had achieved. AmberWave would also help Motorola to produce material of such quality. Assuming that Motorola would get improved transistor characteristics with the supplied material, the new improvements and closer interaction regarding the latest ideas could follow in a subsequent contract.

AmberWave was now a real company, with a customer and a contract. Moreover, some months after this agreement, I was notified by NASA that AmberWave had won an SBIR contract for fabricating high efficiency solar cells. I needed to hire the right people to be my partners. For a while, one of my first PhD students had expressed interest in starting a company after graduation. He had shown the ability to start activities from scratch, as he had helped me form the research group at MIT. With the corporate basic research laboratories only shadows of their former selves by the late 1990s, it was looking as if his only choices would be a faculty position at a research university, or a much more narrow position in development at a major semiconductor company. Both seemed a waste of his talents; he was interdisciplinary and seemed predisposed to pursue vision and practicality simultaneously. After considering more lucrative industrial offers, he became my cofounder in AmberWave.

Let us break from the story here to sum up the changes and their consequences. The mode of executing on the innovation process has changed fundamentally by transitioning it to AmberWave. Whereas before, iterating through Market and Implementation tended to consume few resources, the direct customer interaction now needed time and money. Deriving AmberWave's initial funds directly from the interest of potential customers was money earned the hard way, but the quality of Market feedback and Implementation information could not have been better at this stage. Only by entering into real contractual transactions are a customer's interest and detailed needs truly revealed. The interaction with Motorola made the detailed Market needs much more clear, and it added resolution to Implementation in terms of

AmberWave's business model. AmberWave had to figure out how to make the strained silicon material (wafers) outside MIT for Motorola, thus forcing it to interact with the supply chain of the industry. In turn, both Market and Implementation changed the Technology, because technical development needs changed in priority. Furthermore, the interaction between Implementation and Technology led to the initiation of an intellectual property (IP) strategy for AmberWave, with a view to protecting inventions down the road. Now to resume the story:

> With the Motorola partnership for strained silicon electronics, and the SBIR grant for high efficiency solar cells, it was possible to fund AmberWave "organically" over the next two years. But with a time limit on the government money, AmberWave could not just rely on a single partnership for its future, especially since the ultimate right Market and thus application was unclear at this stage of the innovation process. Would the Motorola partnership last, and could AmberWave avoid being pushed into the unattractive business model of becoming a pure materials supplier of strained silicon? Another option was to evolve AmberWave into an integrated manufacturer of the high efficiency solar cells, which seemed more feasible than doing so in microprocessors, as the capital investment required would be sizable but comparably much less. But how could the company grow organically to such a point, given the high qualification requirements for suppliers to space missions? The market entry hurdles in the case of silicon germanium transistors for wireless communications were high, yet nominally less

than for digital microprocessors. But which technology would the wireless communications industry likely adopt for its future generation of cell phones? It would be foolish to pick one application and Market based only on thinking. Data was needed, and that meant iterating through the Market and Implementation details for all three of these application areas.

Meanwhile, with the SBIR contract due to end in two years, AmberWave had to engage more potential customers. Over that time period, we had conversations or visits with more than 40 companies in the prospective industries. We thus figured out how the incumbent companies in all three Markets were thinking, what their perceived needs were and how they ran their businesses. This also helped provide more information on the Technology specifications the innovation would need to satisfy, and helped us understand the complex supply chains in each industry to identify possible business models for Implementation. At least one major customer in each Market was willing to spend time working with AmberWave. For wireless communication integrated circuits, Qualcomm appeared as a potential early adopter. For high efficiency solar cells, a European company called ASE became a potential customer and partner. And for strained silicon microprocessors, there was the partnership with Motorola. Other interest from the digital integrated circuit industry was slow to develop at this stage, but some of the contacts and the transaction-based learning seemed likely to prove useful at a later stage. Although this learning and iterating in parallel in three potential application areas was exhausting, I hoped that the process would provide the resolution needed to significantly raise the chances of taking AmberWave down a successful innovation path.

In 1999, Motorola encountered with full force the fact that it had missed the boat on the conversion from analog cell phones to digital ones. Shareholders questioned the viability of the incumbent CEO, and Motorola made sweeping cuts across the board in response, including to forward-looking R&D that could lead to new products. Such short-sighted failure to nurture the corporate innovation pipeline was all too common in the late 1980s and throughout the '90s. I had experienced it first-hand at AT&T, and now here was another storied American company doing the same thing. For AmberWave, this was a serious change since future work with Motorola was cancelled. As government funding was not predictable and no other corporate partnerships had yet materialized, AmberWave started to run into cash-flow problems. The company was still small (four people working on AmberWave, one full-time employee). Nonetheless, this size of company required hundreds of thousands of dollars per year to continue, and I had written personal checks to fill the void, but my limited capacity for this type of bridge funding was soon exhausted. I realized that private capital was required to keep AmberWave alive.

We pause again to take stock of the process. While the Technologies for strained silicon and solar applications both progressed steadily in iterations with their respective customers,

AmberWave iterated the full scope of its innovation simultaneously through three Markets directly with dozens of customers. Since real interest from multiple Markets was verified, Implementation became the most uncertain area now. Many possibilities for business models, positions in the supply chains, levels of engineering systems integration, manufacturing set-ups, intellectual property strategies, etc. existed, and they all influenced each other as well as Technology and Market. Innovation iteration was very intense now; iterations happened quickly and on multiple levels.

During these times, Fitzgerald realized that the "focus focus focus" mantra blindly enunciated by venture capitalists is much more nuanced than the statement seems to communicate. For a fundamental advance that can impact multiple markets, gambling on a particular market early without sufficient iteration (i.e. "focus focus focus" on a target market) is as dangerous as working on multiple market applications for too long. For example, in this time period, many experienced entrepreneurs had told Fitzgerald to avoid the digital integrated circuit space since it was not revolutionary enough (recall this is the late 1990s); integrated optoelectronics for telecommunication applications was a much more distant but revolutionary target. Fitzgerald was able to hold off committing to such focus, since it was not apparent to him how one could quickly overcome the very complex technical challenges for integrated optoelectronics, and real customers seemed distant despite the telecom hype at the time. On the other hand, he realized that pursuing multiple applications for too long would drain the company of precious resources. The ideal approach was to carry the Technology, Implementation, and

Market iteration based on quality information far enough so that the probability for the correct choice was increased.

I had been keeping the venture capital option alive in parallel since 1998. By the late '90s, the venture capital industry portrayed itself to be mature and to have a very "mechanical and known" process of investing. I made the rounds to the Boston and Sand Hill Road firms. With MIT and AT&T Bell Labs as brand enhancers, I was able to pitch a number of top firms as well as intermediate, new firms. Although it sometimes seemed that dot-coms could raise funds with little more than a few presentation slides at that time of exuberant capital, I found that a semiconductor company like AmberWave met with a surprising reluctance from venture capitalists. Most "semiconductor" firms they were familiar with were of course the kind without fabrication lines, the chip design houses. The lack of long-term views on semiconductors combined with the dot-com frenzy gave few venture capitalists an optimistic view of AmberWave: why invest in something that was harder to understand than a web page or a company using software to design circuits? One venture capitalist said to me, "Look at this graph", pointing to an exponentially rising curve. "We are making 10x on our money in 18 months. Soon we will be making 10x in 12 months. You guys are building real things that take too long!" I was nearly prompted to ask him if he had considered that he and other investors in aggregate might be creating that curve. But I kept quiet and concluded I had to find venture investors with more grounding in reality.

This happened as the result of a hallway conversation at MIT. I ran into an alumnus from my undergraduate fraternity who was about ten years my senior. He was a technology journalist in the process of becoming a venture capitalist. When I mentioned that I was a founder of a budding company he asked me to pitch his firm, and I took the invitation.

The strategy I would present was one that had emerged from the repeated iterations of Technology-Market-Implementation across the three application areas. The plan was for AmberWave to concentrate first on the solar cell application to drive the materials production early, then use the profits generated by that business to leverage the much larger capital investments required for the electronics applications — whether it was digital electronics based on strained silicon, wireless electronics based on silicon germanium, or both. Not only did the electronics applications require more capital, they required high-volume production with tight quality control. It made sense to master some fundamental and potentially shared production issues in a smaller volume market first, and it also made sense to fund an enterprise that could amplify later investments by its own profits.

But when I pitched this strategy to the people at the venture firm, I found it did not make sense to them — not in the framework of their incentives and priorities. Being careful with cash was not an objective; investment capital was cheap and abundant, and venture capitalists were incentivized to place large bets. A strategy that included organic capital generation was perceived as diminishing their potential return on investment despite the correspondingly reduced risk. The high efficiency solar market alone would not justify a large investment in AmberWave, since the total end-market size at the time was only a few hundred million dollars. The total end-market sizes for wireless and digital electronic applications were approximately 10 billion dollars and 200 billion dollars, respectively. In addition, as popular as solar technology is today, it was not considered an area viable for investment in 1999. It was a failed market from the 1970s, and since cheap capital was encouraging herd investing, I received chuckles from the alumnus' firm when I mentioned it as a business to build on. Ironically, if solar had been pursued then, AmberWave would have drawn much interest as a viable high-efficiency solar company in 2005.

Despite the resistance, I was able to raise a seed round of financing at the end of 1999. This alleviated the cash flow problem and allowed some time to recruit a CEO and additional personnel to advance the company, and therefore the iterative innovation process. The venture investors wanted to see both electronic applications pursued, but also the highly speculative integrated optoelectronics application for the burgeoning telecom bubble. The solar cell application was annihilated. One positive feature of inexpensive capital was that three application areas could be pursued for a little while longer. Eventually, more customer interaction and expression of interest made the two electronics areas appear the most promising. The materials for integrated optoelectronics were still fairly incompatible with current manufacturing practices. Building a fabrication facility, even in the age of cheap capital, was beyond financial reality. I had enough influence in the company to narrow the short-term objectives to digital and wireless integrated circuits, and to push integrated optoelectronics into an "R&D pipeline". The ability to entertain such a long-term technology pipeline within a start-up company was again a direct consequence of inexpensive capital. Everyone, including investors, was confident that more capital would be available if the results of the technology were promising.

As a venture-backed company now, AmberWave needed to be made to look like one. The venture capitalists and I recruited a CEO who was a VP in a large corporation. With this CEO in hand, and with the beginnings of a typical-looking management structure, AmberWave appeared more substantial and we then raised a much larger round of venture capital. That investment allowed us to build a small R&D and pilot production facility for the engineered materials that were the basis of all three market directions. The construction of the facility kept business-model options open, although it implied a direct continuation of the business model I had converged on with Motorola: engineering services and materials supply to allow a semiconductor partner to produce advanced integrated circuits with AmberWave's technology.

Breaking with the story for a moment, note that before the infusion of venture capital, AmberWave's purpose was the execution of the iterative innovation process in the Market, not the building of a company in accordance with the prevailing notion of venture-backed entrepreneurship. A fine small to medium-sized solar company could have been created with a small investment, and that was in fact what the innovation process was pointing to. However, the cash flow problems forced the innovation and the innovators into another organizational transition. Once venture capital was accepted, the financing itself became an integral part of Implementation, precluding convergence on innovation outcomes that could not produce the expected return. Absorbing tens of millions of dollars in risk capital and handing ultimate control from the innovators to the financiers changed Implementation, which was now influencing Market and Technology more strongly than the other way around. Although we do not intend to cover it in detail here, the technological development for progressing along engineering paths in solar, integrated optoelectronics, digital integrated circuits, and wireless circuits are quite different. Due to limited resources and time, the iterative cycle was reduced to the most viable possibilities of digital and wireless electronics, given the size of investment.

I was now Chairman of the Board at AmberWave. As we were building our R&D/pilot facility, hiring personnel and pursuing new customers in the two electronics areas, I thought about how the company was risking all on a certain vision of the future, and that this future had narrowed realistically to the two product areas where it had to contend with big players. Since a back-up strategy seemed warranted, I pushed for building an intellectual property base that would cover all areas of potential products.

In the late '90s, the role of intellectual property in high technology, and in particular in semiconductors, began to shift in response to structural changes that had taken place in the industry. The shrinking of basic research investment by large corporations, the increase in private equity investment, and the rise of outsourced manufacturing by foundry operations all contributed to this shift. As things had stood, most people in the semiconductor business were either formerly or currently employed by one of the larger companies, and therefore the prevailing attitude towards intellectual property was the common big-firm one of "patent when the product goes to market". I had seen this strategy at AT&T. Despite AT&T's massive patent portfolio, it could not afford to patent every idea that any researcher conceived of. Over time, a process was established that favored ideas closer to commercialization. Thus, most participants in the semiconductor industry at the turn of the millennium did not patent in a timely manner, i.e. at the point of actual invention. Some start-up companies had shifted to a timely-patent strategy, but few were doing so at the process level of integrated circuits. All incumbents generally believed that important process advances at this stage in silicon integrated circuits could only be achieved by large semiconductor companies. This proved to be a significant oversight.

Since AmberWave was risking all for its future anyway, why should it not pursue timely patenting, i.e.

patent the inventions in AmberWave right away? After all, if the vision of the future turned out to be wrong and AmberWave's technology would be bypassed by the semiconductor industry, the company would fail anyway. If it was true, however, that AmberWave's technology would inevitably become adopted across the industry, timely patenting would become a form of insurance policy. The initial venture capital could support the development of a patent portfolio. As the nature of AmberWave's revenue streams would become more resolved, it could abandon patents from unpromising revenue paths. These realizations strongly influenced the company's patent strategy, and in fact AmberWave formed an "IP Group" responsible for establishing patents around inventions for its future vision. This was not as easy to execute as it may seem, since expert personnel were scarce and busy with making the current inventions scalable to larger volume as well as creating the new processes and materials for future inventions. Thus, an active management process was necessary to create the timely patent portfolio in parallel.

The structure of the patent portfolio was influenced by the structure of the semiconductor industry. As the quote "Real Men have Fabs" reveals (it's attributed Jerry Sanders, cofounder and former CEO of the big chipmaker AMD), AmberWave's strategy for patenting had to be very different from that of incumbent companies with manufacturing facilities. AmberWave needed to think carefully about its likely business model as well as the structure of the industry. For example, it was clear to me that our current engineering services model would enable new generations of integrated circuits in a multi-billion-dollar market. To extract the proper payment for our services, royalties would have to be collected at the level of chip revenue. Collecting the royalties at the materials or process level would leave all value to the incumbent industry, since the final chips are worth approximately 100 to 1000 times as much as the material they are built on. In the past, it was the technology of building the chips that made them faster, whereas now it would be AmberWave's materials innovation. That fact, however, would do nothing to change the existing global semiconductor supply chain and its value extraction points. The weakest level of the supply chain with respect to patenting is the process level, since there are many ways to change a process and still produce the same kind of final chip. These considerations lead to the conclusion that AmberWave had to develop a patent portfolio that reached all the way up to the chip level, covering materials, process, devices and circuits. To build the strongest portfolio possible, R&D had to produce prototypes of the inventions at each level of the semiconductor supply chain.

Let's record another crucial entry in our innovation log book. Setting up the IP Group for timely patenting early, developing the strategy of patenting vertically up the entire silicon industry supply chain, and guiding the execution of this strategy was the result of another major iteration between Market, Technology and Implementation. The iterative process went as follows. Interacting with the Market, Fitzgerald deduced both the opportunity and the need for the IP strategy to enhance AmberWave's Implementation (as a small company) in the form of an insurance policy for protecting its Technology, as well as to enhance the Implementation of the engineering services and materials supply business model to extract the appropriate value for its Technology from the Market. The Implementation of the IP strategy itself required detailed Technology understanding across the industry's supply chain, from materials synthesis to chip design, for mapping it onto AmberWave's Technology — which then guided the right kind of Technology inventions to be deliberately made for becoming the elements of AmberWave's IP portfolio, an important part of the firm's overall Implementation.

Connections through venture capitalists as well as through the MIT network enabled our CEO and me to speak with high-level officials at AMD. A collaboration and license agreement was eventually reached, and AmberWave was able to work with AMD in the framework of the engineering services and materials supply model. Intel had been interested in AmberWave as early as 1998, through its then newly formed venture capital arm, Intel Capital. We had explained the benefits of strained silicon in detail over the period of a couple of years, but several meetings did not result in any agreement. After seed-round financing, our investors did not want strategic investment from an industry participant such as Intel. Beyond the vertically integrated microprocessor companies, connections were made to the leading-edge chip design companies (the kind without fabrication lines) on top of the disaggregated silicon industry supply chain. In addition, AmberWave established a partnership with one of the major silicon foundries, UMC in Taiwan, for outsourced chip production. This partnership was also based on the engineering services and materials supply model. Many other semiconductor companies from the U.S. and around the world eventually established activity with AmberWave in this business model. In all cases, the partners were notified of AmberWave's intent to collect future revenue based on chip royalties. Virtually all of these companies were interested in strained silicon technology for digital applications, that is, the next generation of silicon process technology required for advancing digital integrated circuits. Although Qualcomm had initially driven the wireless direction, it was becoming clear that AmberWave's technology development path was too slow for Qualcomm's needs. Consequently, digital integrated circuits became our market, although some R&D activity on integrated optoelectronics was still carried out in the background.

As we worked with our international set of partners, we acquired an integrated picture of the silicon industry far better than most large semiconductor companies. The reason for this was simple: large semiconductor companies at this time did not work closely with each other on key forward-looking technology advances. True, there was the industry's "Roadmap" of future technologies needed, which Intel developed with other large semiconductor companies. But the Roadmap would not include a technology unless it was either predictable or universally acknowledged to require development efforts that one company could not finance alone. AmberWave began working with the Roadmap committee to introduce strained silicon as a viable technology for meeting future needs of the industry, and the technology would subsequently appear on the Roadmap.

Our global partnerships across the silicon electronics industry also modified the nature of the technology that we pursued. We naturally had to respond to the detailed engineering requests from our customers. The initial strained silicon technology used tensile strain and resulted in a 20–30% performance gain for electronic devices. However, as early as 2001, my research showed compressive strain can result in up to a 1,000% gain in performance. Despite this order-of-magnitude technology advance, it became clear that our partners, and our company AmberWave, wanted to pursue the more incremental approach of working with the 20–30% gain since the compression technology was less developed. Our partners wanted to be educated on the capabilities of the future compression technology, but both the partners and our company were more interested in applying the more developed approach at that time.

The heat on AmberWave in the marketplace increased in 2001 when IBM announced that *it* had discovered strained silicon technology, and that this technology was a key to making integrated circuits in the future. Our own progress wasn't widely known, as we had always kept the engagements with our partners confidential through non-disclosure agreements. With the announcement from IBM, we needed to make a key strategic decision: go public about what we had, or remain silent. We decided to go public and issued a press release stating that my invention of strained silicon technology could be obtained by working with AmberWave, and that AmberWave was very glad IBM recognized the importance of these advances. A stunned IBM corrected its original press release and clarified that IBM did not invent strained silicon, but would be the first to commercialize it.

Meanwhile, Intel was holding its cards tight to the chest, and may well have been surprised by the degree of strained silicon process technology being developed by an array of companies at that point. However, according to Intel's published accounts, Intel had not been pursuing strained silicon technology but rather was pursuing one of the standard industry Roadmap technologies called raised-source-drain, and therefore unusually, Intel was somewhat behind in the strained silicon race. As it turned out, the raised-source drain technology was Intel's accidental path to compressive strained silicon.

Tracking AmberWave's innovation iterations during this period, we note that real customer transactions have permanently converged the innovation cycle onto the Market of digital integrated circuits. The iterations between Market and Technology were now happening rapidly, since the Implementation of AmberWave's business model as an engineering services and materials supply company provided an optimal feedback mechanism. Engagement with customers, suppliers, and other participants eventually influenced AmberWave's investors as well. The transactions with customers resulted in focusing the Technology, choosing the right "bite-sized" advance for the customers and leaving the more advanced Technology, compressive strain, for the future. Finally, the innovation iteration involved enough people and companies that a tipping point occurred with the announcement by IBM. Although AmberWave was not involved with IBM at that time, the people within IBM who seeded its development of strained silicon were from Stanford, where they worked with the professor who followed Fitzgerald's initial breakthrough at AT&T Bell Labs. Also, while they were performing research and migrating to IBM's innovation environment, AmberWave had been seeding the marketplace by educating semiconductor companies around the world about strained silicon technology.

Intel announced in 2002 that it, too, would use strained silicon in production. AmberWave had not realized at the time what the large integrated microprocessor companies like Intel, AMD and IBM had realized: the general industrial roadmap of shrinking transistors and putting more into chips (i.e. Moore's Law) would be coming to an end without some way of improving the performance of the tiny, leading-edge next generation transistors. This swept AmberWave and strained silicon into the center of the high performance integrated circuit industry. Intel said it would release strained silicon integrated circuits in 2004. Between 2002 and 2003, AmberWave's partners were fully engaged, more than ever, in determining how to incorporate strained silicon into their future integrated circuits. However, as 2004 approached, Intel started revealing the details of its process, which was based on the raised-source-drain compressive strain process. The industry became paralyzed, essentially waiting to see what Intel's process was so that they could follow.

To me, it became clear in 2003 that AmberWave would have to change its business model for continued convergence of the innovation. From 1997 to 2003, AmberWave had been growing with the market, both in engineering services revenue and in materials sales revenue. However, when it became clear that the high performance digital integrated circuit industry would need to adopt strained silicon, there was no way that AmberWave could meet the demand for materials or services. A single silicon fabrication facility at the time would require between 500,000 and one million strained silicon wafers per year, whereas our facility could produce 3,000 and our outsourced supply chain could produce tens of thousands of wafers per year, but not millions.

I was convinced in late 2003 that since Intel was going to release the first strained silicon integrated circuits, AmberWave had to follow one of two paths: license to Intel, or manufacture its own integrated circuits based on strained silicon. Both paths represented increased risk in the eyes of the investors. After all, strained silicon was the new hot technology and they happened to be invested in the early company in that field. Revenue had been increasing and along with it the company's value. Why rock the boat? My strongly held view was that the boat was going to be rocked, if not swamped, regardless, and we needed either to raise investment for producing our own product, or shrink the company and marshal remaining resources for litigation. Since the investors disagreed at the time, I resigned from the AmberWave board in protest. Weathering the storm in a marketplace that suddenly turned competitive is something large companies might have been able to do, but not a start-up like AmberWave. I moved on to other innovations and founding other start-up ventures.

AmberWave was eventually forced into the intellectual property model in 2006, after initial contacts with Intel about licensing led to an exchange of lawsuits. AmberWave was willing to go on helping semiconductor companies develop strained silicon technology, but customers now feared AmberWave's strong intellectual property portfolio, and also began to experiment with Intel's process. As it turned out, Intel could implement its process internally, for it had the market dominance and the resources. It could circumvent the need for a materials supply company by incorporating the required capital-equipment expansion into its manufacturing facilities. Thus, the completion of the innovation iteration had to occur within Intel, forcing the business model change within AmberWave. Other players could not implement such a process from scratch, not without Intel-sized resources and without strained silicon knowledge. Therefore, it was clear that Intel would be manufacturing strained silicon integrated circuits alone for years before the competition caught up, and therefore also had come the conclusion that AmberWave needed to obtain license revenue for its Technology from Intel. In 2007, Intel announced the licensing of AmberWave's strained silicon technology. Later, the portfolio was also licensed to a foreign semiconductor manufacturer.

The outcome was quite different from what I had envisioned at the start. I had expected to see strained silicon put into chips by AT&T, and then by a start-up, via any of several routes other than the one the innovation took at the end. But things turned out well after all. Intel went forward. AmberWave realized returns and is still in business, working with other materials technologies. I learned a tremendous amount that I could carry into new endeavors. And the innovation is on the market, delivering benefits that will grow with new uses and follow-on innovations in years to come.

Near the end of this story, the delay in shifting business model was nearly catastrophic for AmberWave. Between 2003 and 2006, the company pursued a business model not focused on the way the innovation iteration would finish. This delay no doubt cost the start-up company tens of millions of dollars in resources, and could have closed the window for strained silicon licensing. Fortunately, the patent portfolio and importance of the technology could compensate for the delay in the final innovation iteration.

We have previously mentioned the difficulty of running the entire innovation process in a single organization. The strained silicon case offers a window into the comparative roles of corporate basic research laboratories such as Bell Labs in its time, and companies that concentrate more on what comes after the research. During the 1980s and early 1990s, which marked the end of the era dominated by large incumbent firms, organizations like Bell Labs still excelled at the first part of the innovation process, whereas newer companies like Intel focused on the second part. The AmberWave story took place during the time period when large vertically integrated companies were giving way to entrepreneurship and "institutional venture capital". The Bell Labs-MIT-AmberWave-Intel progression thus reflects the innovation pipeline in transition from around 1990 to 2005. Today, Intel is required to do more basic research itself, and has built university consortia like SRC-MARCO to help with the very earliest stages of the fundamental innovation process.

With the strained silicon story now complete, we would like to highlight a few final points by briefly drawing from our experiences with the iterative innovation process in one follow-on and two other cases. We had selected strained silicon for the detailed story because it is highly unusual to have a ground-level view of the full fundamental innovation process from its earliest beginnings to end, from the person centrally involved all the way, across several organizations. Typically, records of fundamental innovations that do not have such ongoing involvement of the same innovator tend to become "linearized", at least in parts. A linearization of our story above would look something like this: AT&T research results in the strained silicon discovery; MIT research discovers materials and process solutions for strained silicon; the MIT start-up AmberWave Systems Corporation commercializes strained silicon technology; and Intel licenses AmberWave's technology. That may suffice for some historical purposes, but for understanding the details of the innovation process and its implication for individuals, organizations, and governments, such historical narratives offer little insight. We hope you have gotten a clear and strong sense of the utterly non-linear messiness of the innovation process, and how Market,

Technology, and Implementation interact as the innovators iterate. The story also drives home the meta-stable nature and sensitivity of the process.

The iterative innovation process is optimized with respect to time and resources when it follows the path of sequentially reducing the next highest uncertainty — regardless of whether the process starts in Market, Technology or Implementation — and when the uncertainty reduction is based on quality learning and abstraction. Efficiency is correlated with the skills of the innovators and with access to quality information on which the learning is based. Iteration efficiency is positively impacted by environments where high quality knowledge and experience across all three areas is dense and readily shared, such as the original AT&T Bell Labs, where early fundamental innovation narrowed in on a research direction quickly. But even there, the thoroughness required for performing "excellent research" could not be cut short. The environment of pre-venture-capital AmberWave was also very efficient for iterating in a later stage, thanks to its flexibility in interacting with many customers in different Markets. But again, the thoroughness required for quality transaction-based learning could not be cut short. AT&T Bell Labs and pre-venture-capital AmberWave stand out in our story for innovation efficiency, although at different stages of the process. What these environments had in common was that both were dominantly populated by talented innovators, and the innovators were inherently placing priority on serving the iterative innovation process.

We could derive confirming data from our experiences with Innovation Interface, the university-industry mechanism in which we form teams of bright young innovators from the upcoming generation to innovate together with experienced innovators and companies. Having done this for innovations in areas from consumer goods to large-scale industrial infrastructure, and across several industries, our experiences with different team compositions confirm the importance of an environment in which the innovators follow the innovation process naturally.

As a corollary, innovation efficiency is negatively influenced when people whose thinking and/or incentives are not attuned to the iterative innovation process have a major impact. In the strained silicon story, this was the case at AT&T when management could not aid commercialization, driving Fitzgerald into the transition to MIT for continuing the innovation process. Progress was hampered through the period leading up to the transition, until it had gotten to the point where a move seemed the only viable choice, and then the transition took time and considerable effort. Later, AmberWave was majorly impacted by the venture investors' dismissal of high-efficiency solar cells, the very option that the company's iteration process had converged on as the best entry market in that case. Although Fitzgerald chose to take venture capital at the time, we are in a very fortunate position to share with you something of an "alternative ending". With more fundamental research, Fitzgerald could restart the solar cell technology development outside AmberWave. Based on his past experiences, he took quite a different financing approach this time. Here is Fitzgerald's abbreviated story of the restarted solar cell innovation path. He omits the name of the "company" here due to confidentiality reasons at the time of writing:

Five further years of fundamental research proved that high quality optical materials could be integrated, allowing high efficiency solar cells to be much lighter and lower cost than existing high efficiency cells. We formed a start-up company to push for the final iterations to commercializing the innovation. Exactly at this time, the price of oil surged past $100 per barrel and eventually to $140. Venture capitalists had by then been trying to create a market for solar investments, and therefore a long line of venture firms wanted to fund the company. But the company did not entertain any equity investment. Why? This time, instead of letting contemporary forces drive the decision making, we wanted to continue relying on iterative innovation and the longer view it provided. As the company advanced the technology and fed that information back into cost models, the models showed that a long lasting solar bubble would be a prerequisite for reaching a mass-market or even wide-market application. The firm's high efficiency solar technology would not come down in cost close to the costs of conventional silicon solar cells within the next five years.

Iterative innovation was forcing the company up-market, making the innovation head towards the niche markets in which the properties of the technology are highly valued. Government is a dominant customer in these niches, and indeed, the innovative cells won a government contract to produce high efficiency, low cost, light cells. Note that in this market, "low cost" is still an order of magnitude higher than that of conventional silicon mass-market solar, but far lower cost than the incumbent high efficiency technology. The convergence of the innovation in this direction was clearly pointing to high-end markets that were lucrative in margin but not very large in total size. Calculations showed that absorbing venture capital, in the prevailing institutionalized methodology, would have eventually killed the company. However, the bootstrap approach with small investments from the company founders showed early returns that far exceed the 20-year average return from venture capital investments.

This brief example shows the benefit of performing the iterative innovation process until the end, while avoiding the potential distortion from financing that is not attuned to the innovation process. But to show that outside financing also can have the positive effect of jump-starting iterative innovation, we would like to share the following experience.

In this case, an inventor had been working on the general idea that there should be a low-cost way to make semiconductor memory devices in much the same way that DVDs are made. The memory end-product wouldn't use optical storage and retrieval as a DVD does; it would be strictly electrical; the interest here was in adapting the manufacturing process. DVDs are very simple and cheap to make, with few process steps and few mask levels. The inventor had developed and filed for patents on a number of technologies over five years, at first with very little capital, and then with a small amount of angel financing. Working alone, he tried to make further progress, but in the context of our innovation model, he could not move towards a real innovation since he had neither Market nor Implementation knowledge.

Recognizing some potential but also recognizing that the work would go nowhere without other expertise, a venture capitalist contacted an experienced innovator to participate in creating a new company around the inventor's concepts. The innovator brought some Market knowledge, but more important for this task, Implementation knowledge. As he sifted through the array of loosely related concepts and patents aimed at "low cost" memory, his Implementation knowledge revealed that most of the inventions and ideas were not relevant, or necessary, for achieving the goal. In fact, there was just one patent with one concept that survived this stage of iteration. The key pieces of Implementation in this case were knowledge about the connection between cost and manufacturing processes, as well as the design. Combining the market goal of low cost memory with these two pieces of information, one design concept emerged as the potential key innovation with which to proceed. With this focus as a result of the first pass at iterative innovation, a second pass now revealed that 80% of the cost savings would be achieved by implementing the design based on the one patent, and in addition, the prototype could be produced by partnering with existing manufacturing environments.

This story is still under way as we write. We shared it to show that when parties are attuned to the iterative innovation process, as this venture capitalist was, they can step in and help greatly.

Before an actual iterative process began, the array of concepts implied that new factories and tools might need to be built. The innovation iteration started from the Implementation side, identifying the one out of many Technology pieces with potential. Having now shown examples of innovation processes started from both Technology and Implementation, we would like to round out this chapter with a brief example of one started from the Market side. This is about a company called The Water Initiative:

> The founding concept in The Water Initiative was that population growth and economic growth worldwide was creating a large market for point-of-use (POU) water purification. The economies of many developing countries have lifted large numbers of people out of poverty to the extent that they can pay for things they once couldn't, and in many cases one of the first things they would like to have is potable water, without having to boil it or take other onerous steps. There may be water-system pipes into homes and buildings but one still ought to purify the water; hence the Market. Numerous companies had entered this space but none had been able to scale to the extent of the founder's vision. A closer inspection, from the viewpoint of the Market, revealed why. Most of the companies followed a business model and a Technology path in which: (a) a particular point-of-use technology was sold to whomever would buy it — that's "technology push", which will capture some amount of market share but miss the buyers who can't use or don't prefer what is offered — or, (b) a one-system-that-fits-all was offered at

high cost, which would win in very few markets. Customers either couldn't afford it at all, or would pick one of the lower-priced alternatives that worked for them.

These previous errors were recognized in the first cycle of iteration, leading to the realization that further iteration for different markets would require several things. First, a database of the myriad existing component technologies for POU water purification, to make the Technology part visible and available for iterative innovation. Second, a system to understand the exact local Market needs and behavioral patterns regarding water usage. Third, a system to determine the appropriate business model for Implementation within the local societal and economic parameters. The Water Initiative was developing the methodologies for iterative innovation within a service company aimed at the following goal: being able to work in any region worldwide, to develop the needed Technology and business model for quickly delivering innovative products that actually meet the specific local Market needs and Implementation requirements.

The process set up by the company was successful in the first regional area tried, in Mexico. The core of the process was a method for working with the local community to determine the local Market needs and identify a business model, while iterating with the Technology team. This led to a device which purifies the local water at a cost that people in the area can afford, yet allows margin for a sustainable business. The device is a free-standing unit to which a supply pipe is connected; potable water comes out of the tap, and the user typically leases the unit by paying an affordable amount monthly. At the time of this writing, the innovation was spreading rapidly in the pilot region, and the company was focusing on repeating the process in a new geographical region.

We hope the stories in this chapter have given an in-depth understanding of how iterative innovation is done in real life. You also have seen examples of how the environment for innovators — the innovation "system" or "pipeline" — can affect the process for better or worse. We now turn our attention to that system. The next chapter traces its long evolution and recent decline. By getting a picture of what has seemed to work and what doesn't, we'll be ready to explore how we might build a better system going forward.

Chapter 6

The American Innovation System

"Good sir, you are an Athenian, a citizen of the greatest city with the greatest reputation for both wisdom and power; are you not ashamed of your eagerness to possess as much wealth, reputation, and honors as possible, while you do not care for nor give thought to wisdom or truth, or the best possible state of your soul?"

Socrates, 399 B.C.,
as told by Plato in "The Apology"

An innovation "system" or "pipeline" is the total environment that nurtures and supports innovation in a society. Some parts of that system are explicitly meant for the purpose, such as research funding. In other cases, the supporting of innovation (or of some key aspect of the innovation process) appears to be more of a fortunate byproduct of certain qualities of an organization, or of the society at large. All parts come together to make up the total system, and it is a system that can be tuned to enhance innovation — but also one that can be inadvertently disrupted, to the detriment of the innovation process.

This chapter reviews how the innovation system in the United States has evolved over the years, as the economy and society have changed. We'll see what made the system once so productive, and how it has deteriorated and been pulled apart in recent times. We begin at the very beginning, with the founding of the United States and the factors that helped to make the country an early breeding ground for innovation.

Early US Innovation: The 'Frontier'

The United States came into being at the very time when the groundwork was being laid for modern technical-industrial innovation and the economic growth that comes with it. This was a happy coincidence that led to a happy marriage: innovation and the U.S. were good for each other. The American Revolution was launched just as the Industrial Revolution was gathering steam. In the summer of 1776, while delegates from the colonies were meeting in Philadelphia to declare independence, James Watt and Matthew Boulton were finishing the first commercial installations of their steam engines in England. That same year, Adam Smith's *Wealth of Nations* was published, with its strong arguments for allowing individuals in free markets to generate growth.

The concept of economic growth was itself then almost as radical an idea as a self-governing democracy. Before that time, although some persons and places had certainly prospered more than others, overall economic expansion had been so negligible that it hardly was even imagined. From the fall of the Roman Empire to the beginning of the Industrial Revolution, annualized rates of growth in the Western world are estimated to have been about 0.25 percent. The possibility of a much more vigorous growth, across a society, was not fully recognized until it began to happen. And when growth did occur it was clearly tied to innovations: either to new forms of Technology like the steam engine, or to new forms of Implementation like the factory system with its division of labor, which Adam Smith illustrated in his famous example of the pin factory.

Thus the stage was set, and the new United States turned out to be an ideal environment for enacting the drama. Without the state directing life, and with very few vestiges of a landed aristocracy, political and personal liberty went hand in hand with economic liberty and the liberty to tinker — a quaint term for real-world experimenting with scientific and technical ideas that is close to what we now call iterative innovation. Among the nation's founders, famous tinkerers ranged from Jefferson, an aristocratic plantation owner, to Franklin, a self-made man of the city. Of course there were similar types in other countries but the freedom of the new country seemed to call forth a profusion of them.

The egalitarian nature of the society had another profound effect. When Alexis de Tocqueville visited the U.S. in the 1830s, he was struck by the proclivity of Americans to "constantly form associations" among themselves, for every purpose from civic and charitable ventures to arts and entertainment. "Wherever at the head of some new undertaking you see the government in France, or a new man of rank in England, in the United States you will find an association", he wrote. He also noted that one purpose stood out above the rest: the forming of associations for industry and commerce, "in which all take part". In the terms of this book, we would say that the vast and burgeoning network of "associations" did several things. It created a variety of settings for transactional learning. It helped to produce a society full of people with hands-on experience at turning ideas into practical applications, across a range of disciplines. And at the center of the hive was the paramount activity, the formation of wealth-creating businesses.

Time and again the result was not just invention, but innovation. Robert Fulton invented many things but not, as is sometimes believed, the steamboat. His contribution was to build a reliable boat and start the world's first successful steamboat service, proving the viability of this new mode of transport. The telegraph was co-invented by multiple inventors across the U.S. and other countries at around the same time, but as the historian Harold Evans has noted, it was Samuel Morse who made the most difference because "He *innovated* the telegraph". Morse completed the innovation with Implementation and Market features like his Morse Code, which came to be nearly universally used, and took other needed steps to bring the invention into wide use.

The impact of the innovations that poured forth in the 1800s was incalculable. Cyrus McCormick, a farmer himself, spent more than a decade iterating his mechanical reaper to near-perfection before selling it beyond limited test markets — and then he mass-marketed it to a staggering effect. He was voted into the French Academy of Sciences for "having done more for the cause of agriculture" than anyone; among other things, the efficiency of his innovation helped to trigger the global shift of labor away from farming, and speeded the westward expansion of the U.S.

That westward expansion, in turn, became another enabler of innovation. If it is true that immigrants tend to be among the most dynamic and adventurous of people, because of their willingness to leave a familiar homeland, then America had an advantage in this regard even from colonial times, having been a society largely built by immigrants. The sheer openness of the country, both in the physical sense of its being sparsely settled and in the societal sense of its having no long-established hierarchies or codes of conformity, created a "greenfield" setting attractive to those who wished to shape new orders of things. Then the opening of the Western frontier doubled the effect. Here was another wide-open space. Even as new arrivals from overseas kept coming in, many who were already settled in the East were stirred to pick up and move on. Frederick Jackson Turner's Frontier Thesis, put forth in his historical writings, argued that this phenomenon fostered personal and social traits of the kind we now associate with innovation. The westward move also firmly set the pioneer as an iconic figure in American culture; almost everyone wanted to blaze new trails, explore new territory.

The first waves of success in innovation helped to develop and refine the support system for it. As fortunes were made, the U.S. in the mid-to-later 1800s became flush with capital searching for investment opportunities. Long before today's venture capital industry, the young Thomas Edison easily found financing for his first innovative venture, as did many others. But perhaps more important were the opportunities for learning to become a technically oriented innovator grounded in practical Implementation and Markets as well. With the mechanization of society, generations of young people grew up around machine shops, or as do-it-yourself mechanics on farms, or (like Edison) working with telegraphy equipment. The young Andrew Carnegie worked as a factory hand, then as a telegrapher and a secretary in business offices, which led to his being personally mentored in business and investing — all before he was out of his teens. Though never a "steel man" in the sense of being technically skilled at working with the metal, he later advanced mass-production steelmaking by knowing the Market well — his early business experience was in the railroad industry, the prime customer for steel — and by innovating in Implementation: he founded a steel company equipped with the latest technologies for efficiency, built it into the prototypical vertically integrated corporation by owning everything from iron and coal mines to the rolling mills at the end of the production process, and even invested in bridge-building to demonstrate the metal's value for that end-use.

And long before the term "spinout company" was in vogue, the new industrial enterprises became learning grounds for people who would leave to develop their own innovations. Henry Ford, a mechanically adept farm boy who also apprenticed at machine shops, broadened his skills by working at Edison's company, then like his predecessor easily found investors when he left to go into auto making. (An iterative process which, by the way, took 10 years before the groundbreaking Model T arrived on the market).

In short, in the United States, the number of individuals capable of industrial-age innovation became high. This trend was augmented by another development in the support system, the widespread founding of colleges with a practical orientation. Many were started under the federal Morrill Act of 1862, under which the states opened institutions to promote agricultural learning and the "mechanic arts". What would become the most notable of the new schools of this era was the Massachusetts

Institute of Technology. Though now known for research as well as education, MIT was for many years essentially a practical training school for vocational engineers in a variety of fields. (The same would later be true of the university Carnegie founded, now Carnegie Mellon, which began in 1900 as "Carnegie Technical Schools").

However by the early 1900s it was becoming clear that more emphasis was needed, throughout the country, on basic scientific research. Despite having many distinguished scientists the U.S. had not been a leader in this area, and by now the basic physical sciences had advanced greatly. Deep theoretical understanding was complementing and demystifying the empirical "black arts" by which most fields of engineering had long operated. Research was opening up new fields while enabling practical innovators to solve problems more efficiently. Also, disparate technical specialties were growing more unified and interdisciplinary as the common principles that underlay them were discovered.

The American innovation system responded in several ways. Some of the era's industrialists-turned-philanthropists funded research projects directly, such as Rockefeller in medical science and others in emerging fields as wide-ranging as rocketry. Corporate research labs proliferated and some became a locus for basic science within a practical context, notably Bell Labs from the 1920s onward. And some of the vocationally-oriented engineering schools added an increasing research focus, notably MIT. The latter two developments were especially valuable, since as we have seen, scientific research and the practical aspects of its application are all part of the same innovation process and need to be iterated together; thus it helps greatly if knowledge about all is present in the same environment. For a number of years, Bell

Labs, MIT and some other places would constitute optimal environments for high innovation productivity.

During the Depression and war years of the 1930s and 1940s, tight capital constraints and then the exigencies of war would further heighten innovation efficiency by requiring timely convergence on innovations that really worked. Later on — as we also have seen already, and will soon hear more about — market forces would tend to isolate longer-term scientific work from practical, technical expertise and from knowledge of Implementation and Market needs. But let's now return to the 1930s. At that point we are entering modern times, in which we can trace the evolution of the American innovation system through several phases up to the present.

Phases of the Modern US Innovation System: National Focus on Science and Technology, Circa 1930–1950

In the 1930s a seminal figure emerged. He was Vannevar Bush, a brilliant engineer and innovator who was Dean of Engineering at MIT from 1932 to 1938, then director of the government's new Office of Scientific Research and Development (OSRD) in World War II. Bush had previously served in a wartime capacity as a charter member of the National Research Council, which was organized in 1916 to focus scientific and technical capabilities for the country's entry into World War I, then became a civilian entity afterward. With war in Europe now impending once again, he recognized that technology-based innovations would again alter the landscape of combat. (For the detailed story, see Gregg Pascal Zachary's book *Endless Frontier*.)

Bush began urging a new and more vigorous coordinating effort, but World War I had left many U.S. generals with the impression that the "war market" was mature. They regarded Bush's idea that new innovations would change warfare as impractical theory and even worried that scientists would gain undue influence over defense planning. Thanks to a close connection to President Roosevelt and one visionary general, Bush persuaded the President to form a joint military-civilian committee that led to the OSRD. Hundreds of fast-track R&D projects were launched across the country, ranging from the Manhattan Project to the mass production of antibiotics for battlefield medicine. Today, Bush is considered an important factor in the Allied victory in World War II.

Two factors changed the postwar U.S. dramatically. The first was a doctrine that Bush spelled out in his 1945 report to President Truman titled "Science, The Endless Frontier". He noted that technology-based innovation had helped to win the war, and also that much of it was applied work drawing on basic research done years before. (New developments in radar, sonar, and medicines were examples of this). He argued that basic research was clearly the wellspring of the future — both for ongoing defense readiness *and* for peacetime economic growth — and therefore, the government should commit heavily and formally to the funding of basic science, especially at universities.

Today it is hard to believe that there was a time when the U.S. government, and many other national governments, *didn't* invest heavily in scientific research. Yet until well into the twentieth century, the largest item in the federal research budget was agriculture, and even most of that was applied R&D. Bush's doctrine spurred the creation of the National Science Foundation and other agencies that would fund basic research in fields from biomedicine to materials and electronics, and help educate researchers as well.

Bush's vision met with a second factor to create a super-efficient innovation pipeline in the U.S. Whereas other countries such as Germany, the U.K., France, and Japan were set back decades by the destruction of their industrial infrastructures during the war, the U.S. emerged with its industrial system not only intact but stronger than ever. This led to a new phase of the American innovation system.

'Innovation without Competition' in the Age of 'Bureaucratic Capitalism', Circa 1950–1980

Having intact postwar industries while implementing Bush's vision meant that every American company built on fundamental innovations became a virtual monopoly. IBM was office equipment and then computers, Kodak was film, Xerox was copying, and so forth. These virtual monopolies generated capital in a time when capital was fairly constrained. Without serious competition in their end markets, their high margins fed the exploration of science and technology further into the future. Companies could afford to have research labs that looked out five to 10 years or beyond, and their pursuits were initially rewarded with higher growth, resulting in yet more R&D investments. This positive feedback between growth and real R&D allowed the iterative innovation process to take hold inside these large corporations. Technology, Market and Implementation were not only simultaneously present in these companies, but they could also interact intimately during this period. Bell Labs alone produced an impressive run of fundamental innovations, from the transistor to the carbon-dioxide laser to the UNIX operating system.

Furthermore many big corporations of the time either still were, or became, vertically integrated to a high degree. AT&T and its subsidiaries made the telephones that you used and also delivered the service, over company-made systems; IBM would build and sell a computer along with the software. This meant that firms had a wide range of interdisciplinary Technology and Implementation interests. Collaboration between corporations at the basic research level was also possible, since each controlled its own end market. This allowed a "scientific commons" to exist and thrive, where each company invested in scientific and technological advances without having to worry about their investments benefiting competitors disproportionately.

During the postwar growth, MIT and other universities moved farther out on the time horizon with their research. Not being able to compete with corporations on innovation, universities eventually were left out of the overall innovation process as they had no significant Implementation or Market knowledge. However, the universities could produce advanced-degree holders with previous exposure to new scientific advances. They became suppliers of fundamental innovation talent, feeding the Technology side of the corporate innovation process.

Meanwhile, an important reciprocal force existed. The corporations influenced basic research at universities — not in any autocratic or devious way, but in useful ways that helped to keep university science focused on promising areas for exploration. For instance, the government's funding decisions were often guided by monitoring innovation in industry. If a corporate lab announced what it deemed to be an important discovery, or if corporations started exchanging information about a new area of science which they thought could lead to useful innovations, this would be read as a "signal" by government funding agencies. The agencies would then solicit proposals for further research in that area from the universities.

An example of this signaling process was the strained silicon discovery at AT&T Bell Labs described in the last chapter. Through the "scientific commons", scientists at AT&T and at IBM Research excitedly exchanged news about the discovery, and soon afterward the government funded university projects to pursue basic research in strained silicon and silicon-germanium.

One might ask: "Why should the government fund basic research at universities in an area where the fundamental breakthrough has already been made in industry? Isn't this double-funding a waste of money?" Actually it was a brilliant arrangement, for several reasons. First of all, the initial breakthrough in a new field doesn't mean the basic research is done. Usually it opens the door so that research can proceed. Second, at any given time there are countless new lines of research that the government could be funding. If you want to choose the ones with real potential for practical application, the interest of knowledgeable basic scientists at business firms is a pretty good indicator. Finally, at universities, graduate students do much of the work on funded research. Whether their work bears fruit at the time or not, they gain experience in an area considered vital by industry, and when hired by industry are ready to step into the innovation process and contribute.

So everyone benefited, and there were mechanisms for direct interaction about basic research as well. Senior corporate researchers at that time participated deeply in peer reviews and editing of scientific journals. Their constant presence at scientific conferences, and on university campuses, provided further "signaling" to the universities and the government about the directions of basic research and often served as a reality check. Corporate researchers were encouraged to spend significant time on these interactions with the scientific commons, while their lack of needing to accumulate publications as academic currency promoted their objective focus on quality research. This interplay between the corporate innovation process, innovation-relevant government funding and universities underpinned the great productivity of the U.S. innovation system in the postwar decades.

But the system of that era also had weaknesses. While a number of the corporate labs were good at doing basic research and iterating through the early stages of the innovation process, often the corporations themselves were not very good at completing the process. This was especially true if the innovation was so fundamental as to not fit easily into the firm's existing business. AT&T never came close to capturing all the value of the great discoveries at Bell Labs, and didn't profit from integrating many innovations into its operations any more than others did. Xerox's Palo Alto Research Center famously developed many of the elements of a modern, networked personal computer, and even a working computer, but the firm never entered that market successfully. The list goes on. Of course many innovations were completed outside the originating companies, but over time, the failures of originating companies to realize value did not bode well for the future of basic research inside corporations. R&D that was more directly focused on incremental improvement to existing business paid off more reliably.

Also, postwar success greatly reinforced the tendency of large firms to be bureaucratic. Bureaucracy, the setting of specified roles for people and procedures for doing things, is meant to make large organizations efficiently manageable. However its stifling effects had long been noted, and by the later 1950s, in studies like William Whyte's book *The Organization Man*, they were starting to be noted with alarm. Yet increasing specialization became the norm at every level and in every function. Work rules on the shop floor spelled out what skilled craft workers could and could not do. Engineers and MBAs came out of the universities intensely schooled in the theories and formulae of their respective fields of study but little else, and were plugged into slots accordingly. Gradually there came to be less and less room for the interdisciplinary individuals and interaction that are key drivers of the iterative innovation process. Good managers tried to create mechanisms to avoid the pigeonholing effect, but with firms growing more complex as well as large, it was an uphill battle. One of the coauthors of this book, Carl Schramm, has called the entire postwar period the age of "bureaucratic capitalism" in the U.S.

Moreover, although fundamental innovation continued to be a highly iterative process, as it always is, the fact was not always widely recognized. Even the visionary Vannevar Bush did not seem to have grasped it fully. In his landmark report to Truman he stated flatly that "Basic research is performed without thought of practical ends", then went on to imply, in this and other writings, that useful pieces could be selected from a random body of research and developed into products by a process that took hard work, but was more or less linear.

The linear "funnel" model came to be implicit in "innovation management". The general idea was to take the best results that emerged from a very broad Step A of the process (the research), move them to Step B — and if some did not make the transition easily, or couldn't then be moved along to Step C, well, only the fittest survived, didn't they? Prudence dictated that you withdraw funding from the laggards and concentrate it in an ever narrowing set of innovations until some emerged from the other end.

Despite the fact that innovations are not derived in this manner, the structure of the organization took over. By adapting the innovation process to fit managerial needs, instead of adapting managerial methods to fit the needs of the innovation process, corporations gradually ceased to innovate in areas important for future markets. Over time, the low innovation productivity of projects needing long iterative development resulted in assigning researchers to direct development tasks for the end businesses. Internal justification of basic corporate research became difficult. Cost-benefit analyses invariably showed that cutting forward-looking research would not hurt profitability, but rather would increase it. The components were coming into place for abolishing integrated corporate research laboratories, where an application-rich environment allowed interdisciplinary innovators to iterate through Technology, Market and Implementation.

Then the death blow to that system arrived — and to bureaucratic capitalism in the U.S.

'Innovation Absorption'
in the Rise of 'Entrepreneurial Capitalism',
Circa 1980–2000

Countries that had been damaged by World War II eventually rebuilt, and rebounded. Many American firms ceased to be virtual monopolies, as Kodak faced increasing competition from Fuji in film, Xerox saw competition from Canon, and so forth. Other U.S. companies, which had long enjoyed holding a comfortable second or third place in market share after their chief domestic rivals, now found themselves a frantic fifth or a sliding seventh as foreign competitors entered.

Often these competitors used the advances in the scientific commons to create innovative products without the costs of basic research (or more precisely, fundamental innovation research). A lot of their innovations tended to be incremental to medium-range innovations which nonetheless made a decisive difference in quality or price to customers in the marketplace. Many non-U.S. firms, especially Japanese firms during this time, honed their organizations to produce such innovations. Some U.S. corporations, like Intel, realized their focus needed to be on manufacturing and not research in order to maintain growth and profits.

Thus began the depletion of the scientific commons. American firms in the new competitive environment were forced to equal the efficiencies of their competition. This process reached its fullest execution during the late 1980s and into the 1990s, when most basic research was excised from corporate laboratories. Corporations became experts at development, manufacturing, and distribution. Many also found a growth-booster by outsourcing manufacturing to companies that concentrated on it. The forces of global competition thus transformed vertically integrated companies into horizontal companies operating on one level of the supply chain. During this evolution from vertical to horizontal structure, earlier innovations that were stored in the corporate pipelines became impossible to implement within the corporation, and further fundamental innovation was no longer possible as Technology and relevant Implementation knowledge ceased to exist within the corporations.

Along with this transformation came a shift in the structure of capital to support innovation. Although the economy no longer had virtual monopolies generating fantastic earnings, a decrease of government regulations in the U.S. — as exemplified by the portability of pension plans, and the reinterpretation of the "prudent-man rule" for investments by pension funds — increased the mobility of innovators and created pools of capital seeking higher-risk, high-return investment. Much of this capital found its way to start-up ventures based on liberating partially completed innovations from the corporate pipelines where they had been piling up. For instance, the Ethernet networking technology was invented at Xerox PARC and deployed within the facility — but it didn't really take off until the co-inventor Bob Metcalfe left and built 3Com, a venture-funded equipment company that widely promoted the Ethernet standard. That occurred soon after the 1978 revision of the prudent-man rule had expanded the pool of venture capital; many more such examples were to follow.

Spurred on by the Moore's Law paradigm, in which integrated circuits were doubling in transistor density about every two years, risk capital found its way to frozen innovators and shelved ideas throughout the country. As described earlier, the integrated circuit revolution led to the rise of the personal computer and software industries, which increased efficiency throughout the economy. Productivity gains allowed more capital to be generated with less labor. The latter would normally mean job loss, but as the innovations kept coming and new ventures and industries kept starting, many people were instead released from the corporate bureaucracies (which by this point were being drastically scaled down anyway) and found work in new high-growth companies. The rise of "entrepreneurial capitalism" was now in full swing, as described by Schramm et al in the 2007 book *Good Capitalism, Bad Capitalism*.

There were a couple of very important efficiencies in the innovation system of entrepreneurial capitalism that are often ignored. First, the innovators funded by risk capital *at the start of this period* were not neophytes. Whether they were from corporations or from garages, they had Market and Implementation knowledge in addition to their Technology knowledge. If they were missing some key knowledge, they could gain it relatively quickly in places like the Bay Area in California, where there were informal exchanges of information and movements of employees that helped embody all the elements of the iterative innovation process in both innovators and entrepreneurs.

Second, the fact that many of the ideas funded by early risk capital had already been, to some degree, invested in by other corporations, was highly relevant for achieving timely returns. For example, consider this chain of events that occurred even before the system transformation described here: the transistor was invented at Bell Labs in 1947. After some subsequent iteration, co-inventor William Shockley left, and in the 1950s was able to start his own laboratory at Beckman Instruments, an electronics firm in California. A group of employees pursued his transistor work for a while, and then left to become part of another established company, Fairchild Camera and Instrument. There they created a division called Fairchild Semiconductor, focused on the still-new concept of making transistors in silicon. At Fairchild one of the group, Robert Noyce, also began research on silicon integrated circuits. (He is now credited as co-inventor of that technology along with Jack Kilby of Texas Instruments, who worked separately.)

After nearly another decade at Fairchild — which included much further iteration, replete with successes and failures across all three areas of Technology, Market, and Implementation — Noyce and his colleague Gordon Moore left and started Intel in 1968, to make and sell silicon integrated circuits in the ways that they thought best. Net result: If we were to say that anyone who invested early in Intel was smart, we would be right. Those investors were not buying into a raw start-up based on an innovation in the early stages of the iterative process. Most of the work had already been done, *all within the confines of existing companies,* and the innovator-entrepreneurs were now seasoned veterans.

With the expansion of venture capital, and eventually the decline of the corporate labs, similar cases became legend. Key pieces of personal computing technology from Xerox PARC were picked up and innovated to completion: the graphical user interface by Apple, the printing technology that spurred desktop publishing by the start-up Adobe. In the case of strained silicon, Fitzgerald discovered the technology fundamentals after years of research at AT&T Bell Labs before advancing it further at MIT and eventually forming the company that first commercialized the technology, AmberWave Systems. It may have appeared that AmberWave's investors were funding a university innovation from MIT, which to some extent they were, but they were also leveraging previous investments at AT&T. Through much of this period, high returns could be gotten on risk capital that wasn't as risky as it seemed.

The run was exhilarating while it lasted. The information-age growth created in the modified U.S. innovation system of this era more than made up for heavy job and revenue losses in older industries. Now, however, we come to the weaknesses of this innovation system. Whereas the bureaucratic corporations of the earlier period were often good at originating innovation but not at completing it, the new system that emerged was nearly the reverse: good for "absorbing" and completing fundamental innovations, but not so good for originating them.

What about university research? Didn't all of the federal dollars pouring into university labs for basic research, from the postwar years onward, produce hosts of fundamental breakthroughs that were then converted to spinout companies and new industries? In fact, while university research has been very valuable in certain cases, it is curiously given much more credit than it deserves for U.S. economic growth in the late twentieth century. Let us now marshal some evidence.

Studies funded and/or reported by the Kauffman Foundation, which specializes in work involving entrepreneurial growth, have repeatedly indicated that the picture is not as clear-cut as it seems. Among the findings: a number of universities that rank high in federal research funding score low on commercialization measures. A study of over 3,000 research faculty at six leading universities, over a 17-year period, found that nearly two-thirds had never formally disclosed an invention, let alone taken steps to develop it into a true innovation. In surveys conducted at another sample of universities, many faculty reported that patenting, licensing and commercialization was such a hassle that it distracted from ongoing research, and they either stopped trying or did not try. And an economic study found that new high-tech economic activity in university regions did *not* correlate with patenting and licensing rates at the universities.

The Foundation has learned that growth does seem to flourish in regions where universities are embedded in highly networked "ecosystems" of innovative activity, such as the Boston area or the Bay Area. But even in these regions, our own investigations suggest that the stereotypical pattern of university-research-turned-into-spinouts is not the predominant factor. For instance, a famous study by BankBoston financial group in 1997 showed that "MIT-related" companies generated revenues of $232 billion in 1994, an impressive figure equivalent to the GDP of a fair-sized country. People often assume that most of these are venture-funded companies based on MIT research, but although we have not closely analyzed the data, we suspect this is not the case. Many were founded by MIT alumni after graduating; many arose in the time before venture funding was prevalent; and a number of prominent ones that we know of, such as Teradyne (1960) and Analog Devices (1965), were not based on MIT innovation.

At Stanford University, the presumed source of research-based spinouts that have driven the growth of the Silicon Valley/Bay Area, Stanford's Office of Technology Licensing website states the following:

Most "Stanford" start-ups are created by Stanford alumni who graduate and become entrepreneurs; the vast majority of these companies are formed without involving Stanford or Stanford technology.

If asked to list the signature "Stanford" companies, most people would name the three high-impact giants: Hewlett-Packard, Cisco Systems, and Google. HP was started in 1939 by engineering alumni Bill Hewlett and David Packard, with mentoring from the great professor Frederick Terman but not on the basis of university research technology. Cisco was founded in 1984 by Len Bosack and Sandra Lerner, who were members of the IT operations staff at Stanford, not researchers. Sergey Brin and Larry Page were graduate students who developed the Google search engine as an outgrowth of their PhD studies, and this work was indeed part of a research program, funded by the National Science Foundation and other agencies. It can stand as an example of university research leading to practical innovation that pays off.

Overall, however, the report on the U.S. innovation system from about the 1980s onward would read as follows. As corporations moved away from basic research and long-term fundamental innovation, venture capital and start-up firms came to the forefront, but often by absorbing and completing innovations that had languished in the corporate pipelines or were derivatives of previous corporate work. University research kept growing, but as we shall see in Chapter 8, it grew detached from lines of inquiry that could lead to practical innovation. The idea that many great innovations were (and are) sitting inside the universities, trapped and waiting to be sprung free, is not supported by an overall view of the evolving ecosystem.

Furthermore, once venture capitalists and other investors had gotten used to initial high returns in this period, they began to chase it in places where the potential for real innovation and profit did not exist. Now we are getting into the next phase of the system, which takes us to the present day.

The Breakdown of the US Innovation System, Circa 2000–Present

The early portents of system breakdown, which were not evident during the excitement of the late 1980s and the 1990s, can be retraced more clearly today. As the various corporate laboratories dissolved, there was no comprehensive recording of the fate of all the ideas on the vine and innovations in their early stages. Many may have simply been lost; the information is scattered among millions of patents and papers in the literature. Some of this information was moved to universities with the movement of previous corporate laboratory personnel taking faculty positions, but eventually that transition was largely completed. There has been no new source of such innovators, able to join ecosystems and innovate in them — and no new source of innovations developed, from the start, within a setting rich in Implementation and Market learning. As we've just seen, the track record of fundamental innovation starting from universities has been sketchy.

In the late 1990s and early 2000s, huge amounts of risk capital were channeled into Internet-related ventures and the corresponding telecom industry deployments. A number of fateful factors went largely unnoticed. One was that the rapid build-out of telecom infrastructure eerily resembled the speculative over-building of railroad lines in the 1800s, which triggered resulting collapses and panics. Another was that in Web-based ventures, incremental iterative innovation can be done fairly quickly and easily. Feedback on Market forces and Implementation possibilities can be gained directly through the Internet itself.

These dynamics, and the extraordinary level of previous earnings from the Moore's Law paradigm, helped propel investments to create a bubble of fictitious innovations. Nearly every incremental innovation – especially on the Web – was perceived unjustifiably as a fundamental innovation, and each was expected to capture the whole projected market as if there were no competition. An idea plus a set of PowerPoint slides was enough to attract millions of dollars in high risk capital, regardless of the incremental nature of the innovation or the inability to sustain a competitive advantage over time. Based on initial singular successes, these investment patterns were copied for other scientific areas, notably biotechnology, which did not even exhibit the same fundamental innovation and wealth-creation characteristics as information technologies. (See Gary Pisano's 2006 book *Science Business* for an analysis revealing that the biotech pharma sector has so far produced little net actual operating profit as a whole).

The severe market correction of 2000–2001 should have substantially restructured our innovation pipeline, but the desire of abundant capital for favorable returns coupled with the low interest rate policy of the Federal Reserve following the September 11th incident upheld the unrealistic return expectations of an investment-driven market. This investment-driven market then created the follow-on bubbles of real estate and financial derivatives, as discussed in the opening chapter. Risk was evaluated fictitiously as if it were a free variable made to fit the Wall Street and venture capital models, rather than being correlated to actual wealth creation via its only real source: innovation.

Venture capital as a financial industry, which served a very important function by bringing previously shelved information-age innovations to market during entrepreneurial capitalism, was extended by easy credit beyond its original effectiveness as a financial lubricant in helping bureaucratic capitalism transform into entrepreneurial capitalism. Although it should be obvious to anyone observing the start-up situation in recent years that really *new* new things were not being created in general, venture capital continued to seek returns from early stage investments after 2001. But the failures to realize the necessary returns from direct investments in university Technology components — wrongly perceived as "innovations" well under way — eventually became a factor in venture capital retreating to later-stage investments, a trend clearly shown by industry data. This shrank the pool of early-stage capital available to anyone who had started genuine innovation iteration and might be ready for, and in the need of, investment to support continued iteration.

Today the innovation pipeline, including its financial components, is in shambles. Universities are still operating in a 1970s model layered with a 1990s model of easy-credit entrepreneurship on top. The gap between universities and Market, and between universities and Implementation, is large. Corporations, which contain some of the Market and Implementation knowledge, have a Technology time horizon of three to five years at best. Neither universities nor corporations are capable of executing on the medium- and long-term innovation process by themselves, and there are no mechanisms by which they can effectively bridge the gaps between them and do iterative innovation together. Neither organization today is able to create new viable sectors of the economy, nor is there a current home for the iterative process to develop fundamental innovations and the next generation of innovators. In short, universities do not have "shelved fundamental innovations" just waiting to be released into the market, and corporations have evolved into operationally efficient organizations incapable of fundamental innovation.

Sadly, most solutions being proposed or enacted are piecemeal, unable to address the systemic problems. Pouring more money into research will not help much if the overall system cannot do a good job of interactively guiding the research, or capitalizing on it. Trying to foment start-up companies, as many regions have done in the name of economic development, will not help much without a sustained flow of fundamental innovations upon which to build companies that can really make a difference. And simply pouring money into education will not help much without careful thought about what it is, exactly, that future innovators need to know and be able to do.

Let's now proceed to address what a real solution set might look like.

Chapter 7

Building a New Innovation System: The Free Market Side

The innovation pipeline needs to be restructured, not just repaired. A new system must be built which is in line with the realities of the present situation, and appropriate to the yet-unnamed new era that we are entering. If we can arrive at such a system, it will offer the greatest opportunity for real economic growth that we have seen in years. How will this happen? Who needs to do what, and how will each player benefit? Crystal balls are dangerous, but active thinking about various scenarios has to be the starting point. We thus hope that this book, with its clear formulation of the innovation process and the forward-looking considerations in the following pages, will help innovators, investors, corporations, universities and governments to plot potential paths for future high growth.

Our forward-looking discussion addresses two sets of actors, on the "free market side" and the "research and education side", in turn. The free market side is directly concerned with entry of the innovation into the marketplace and it includes three types of actors: individual innovators, free-market investors and corporations. The research and education side is more concerned with the beginning of the innovation pipeline, and includes universities and government funders.

Today, university research typically looks 10 to 15 years or more into the future, whereas few corporations and investors have a time horizon beyond three years. This leaves a huge innovation gap between the "free market side" and the "research and education side" for the 3-to-10 year time window. Iterative innovation needs to occur in this gap as fundamental or medium-scale innovation proceeds.

This chapter is for the actors on the free market side. Recall that our iterative innovation process model did not depend, in its formulation, on any particular environment or other factors that nurture the innovation process. This enabled us to understand the very nature of iterative innovation. To talk about building a new innovation system, however, of course we need to consider the effects of the various environments and nurturing factors. There are three elements that the iterative innovation process needs to draw upon simultaneously, or, using our earlier tree growth analogy, it needs three types of "nutrients":

- innovation skills, which the individual innovator is ultimately responsible for acquiring;
- appropriate innovation investment;
- an environment that allows innovators to focus on the iterative innovation process.

We shall address each, in terms of what the various free-market actors can do to provide the proper nutrients. First, however, we'd like to step back briefly to take a macroeconomic view. We have shown that in the U.S. during its early years, the society and economy as a whole constituted a healthy macro-environment for innovation. What does the macro-environment need to provide in today's world?

The Free Market Side: Macro-Requirements

There is no doubt that a free market economy is the most efficient for innovation. Competition among firms of all types and sizes clearly drives incremental innovation, but it is important to assure that the free market also drives fundamental and medium-scale innovation, rather than driving it out by removing incentives for this longer-term work, or by isolating basic research on non-market islands. Obviously if a competitor makes a "leapfrog" advance, one will have to match it, so that is a form of market incentive for fundamental innovation. But instead of relying on catch-up incentives, it's better to nurture fundamental innovation in the first place, which means enabling the full iterative innovation process to unfold. We have already seen some clues as to what this requires in the macro-context. Innovators have to be able to learn through transactional experiences. And flexible business entities that can adjust to changing markets would also be ideal for iterative innovation within a dynamic setting.

One can definitely say that U.S. corporations adjusted after the global competitive shocks of the 1970s and 1980s. The trouble is, they did not adjust in a way that was most conducive to fundamental innovation. The good news from the macro-view is that they were able to adjust so dramatically at all. They were not held to fixed structures and business methods, or steered arbitrarily into new ones, by national industrial policy or by any inherent characteristics of the nation's economy. Given this latitude, adjustments that are more fruitful for long-term innovation are eminently possible, and one can hope they will be made.

The high rate of start-ups over the past few decades is also a healthy macro-sign. Although start-ups are not an economic cure-all, we have seen that they play vital and essential roles in innovation, and a few implications are worth discussing briefly here. One thing has become quite clear: despite high expectations, very few new companies grow into mass-market industry heavyweights like a Microsoft or Intel. Many just grow to the size they need in order to serve niche markets or parts of certain supply chains, and it is valuable to have a rich assortment of these. But many more new firms, as well as the innovations behind them, either fail or never reach their potential. These too are valuable because they show what does not work (or what could have worked except for such-and-such), and the value can be maximized if a couple of conditions are met.

First, it helps to "fail fast", with minimal expenditure of resources. Following the full iterative innovation process from the start can help greatly, since the process can reveal show-stopping obstacles early in the game, and continued iterative learning relies on frequent and cheap micro-failures to avoid heavy commitment to a wrong path. The second condition is that the value of failure is maximized if detailed information about failures is widely disseminated, or at least widely available. If other innovators and entrepreneurs can know specifically what didn't work in terms of Technology, Market or Implementation, their chances of success are raised and so is overall innovation efficiency. Such knowledge is spread more easily in highly fluid, highly networked innovation communities like the Bay Area or Boston, and this undoubtedly contributes to why these geographic hubs have been on average more efficient in the execution of innovation processes.

Another implication: our strained silicon example showed that the start-up AmberWave was able to do well in the iterative innovation process, which involved many companies in many industries, but Intel certainly gained the most in absolute terms at the end of the process. This exemplifies a complex co-dependency between innovators and existing businesses on the free market side, a co-dependency that contributes to the overall efficiency of the innovation system. Small companies create threats, options, education and de-risking for all active participants in the economy, and are therefore the invisible hand of innovation and growth progression, even with innovations that result mostly in growth for large corporate entities. One caveat is that small innovators won't keep innovating without hope of some sort of reasonable return. Knowing that the nation's economy as a whole has benefited may generate some good feeling, but it surely won't pay the bills. There has to be something in it for the small innovator too — and fortunately, in the U.S., more often than not there is.

The era of entrepreneurial capitalism has created a valuable new toolkit for small company formation and financing despite the negative effects of overextending during the financial bubble. Since the non-competitive environment of the post-WWII era will not return, we need to safeguard these mechanisms and keep refining them. They are essential innovation nutrients on the free market side. We could sum up some of the key macro-factors for a good innovation environment as follows:

- Individual mobility, in terms of both career mobility and ease of learning and exchanging knowledge.
- Ease of organizational transformation.
- Ability to retain earnings from innovative activity.
- The rule of law, and willingness of others to follow the law (for instance in matters like sharing revenues from a licensed technology).

Although times have been difficult, these basic environmental factors are still present in the U.S. Some other nations have long roads to creating environments in which iterative innovation can thrive. Individual freedoms and lawful but highly unregulated environments are best for innovation. Restricting employees to a lifetime of a certain type of work and forcing business models and supply chains upon the market distorts the outcome of the innovation process.

So, at the macro-level, the innovation environment on the market side appears fine as long as we take care to preserve and refine it. Now we turn to what individual actors can do to nurture innovation, starting with the person at the center of the process.

The Individual Innovator

Although we would stop short of telling new and potential innovators that "everything you've heard about innovation is wrong", we are going to recommend preparing yourself and going about your business in some ways that may be rather different from what has been common recently. For our case example, let's assume we have someone who has discovered that she possesses the desire and predisposition to be an innovator. We will discuss later what the education system can do to help this person prepare. For now we focus on the innovator herself, acting freely in the free market, and we will further assume that she already has some medium-term or fundamental innovative idea. For example, she could have just graduated from a university in a technical field where she came across a promising technology that falls into the 3-to-10 year innovation gap.

This fledgling innovator will need to acquire experience in Technology, Market, and Implementation. With some experience in Technology, but no experience in Market or Implementation, going after a university faculty position would not expose our graduate to either in most cases. It is also unlikely that she will find a position in a corporation that allows her to pursue her innovative idea as part of the job, as one of the forward-looking corporate laboratories of the past might have done. An alternative might be to join, or create, a high risk innovative small enterprise — but the innovation isn't far enough along for a small company to pick it up, or for investors to take a plunge on it, especially in this new era when risk capital is hard to get. All that our innovator has so far is an idea, and the desire. What can she do?

One solution is to have an industry job and innovate on the side. Looking back in history, many great innovators have started out this way, from Edison to Henry Ford to Stephen Wozniak working at Hewlett-Packard while he developed initial Apple computer technologies. The path is not easy, but you earn money while gaining experience, and gain contacts as well. By dedicating additional work hours to the innovation and setting aside personal capital, our innovator may have the resources to start a venture in the future. Although she will ultimately need a separate source of capital to support the ongoing iterative innovation process, this seems the best possible way to begin.

The most important task for an innovator with a Technology-based idea is to interact with the Market and Implementation possibilities to start the iterative innovation process. She also needs to build an interdisciplinary skill set and accumulate knowledge in both of these areas. Therefore, the ideal day job will be one that exposes her to the most relevant knowledge, demands the type of skill set that she will need, and even explores unknown areas pertinent to her innovation. The faster she learns, the more efficiently the iterative innovation process can proceed on the side. Obviously, there is some limit in the sense that the innovator will only be qualified for certain jobs. But it is definitely possible to plan some career steps in the direction of increasing one's exposure towards the maximization of interdisciplinary experiential learning. As a point of caution, the innovator should avoid jobs requiring intellectual property or non-compete agreements that could raise a conflict with her intended future business.

As an example, if the innovator has an idea for a new diagnostic method, a first step would be to become employed by a medical device company that does not have a product line for this particular diagnostic field. Moving into different positions over time, like sales or quality assurance, will allow the innovator to integrate more real-world knowledge about the markets, business models, technology, manufacturing, and supply chains in that sector. Along with accumulating knowledge and training her interdisciplinary skills for the future, the innovator will have a chance to build a network of talent that can work with her — from potential cofounders to experts, such as key university professors with domain-specific knowledge.

By developing and nurturing the innovative idea in the experiential context of relevant Technology, Market and Implementation, the innovator has already started the iterative innovation process. It is highly likely that by starting in this manner, the original idea will be significantly altered. This may even encourage her to leave that particular company and move to a company in a sector more related to the altered idea. Such activity by individual innovators increases the overall efficiency of innovation in the economy.

Beyond the possibility of starting her own venture, her potential innovations could also be of interest to the company in which she is employed. Thus, more options are created since she can decide to either work within the company to innovate, if the culture of the company permits, or to break out on her own, possibly even forming an early partnership with her former employer. In an era when capital is highly constrained, having all these options is very valuable. If this outlined path results in the innovator or a group of innovators forming a new enterprise, ideally the combined personal savings and weekend time are sufficient to de-risk the concept over a year or two. It is unlikely that the innovator can afford to give up her industry job at this point, so she will have two jobs for some time, and managing that process has consequences both for the potential new company and her personal life. The important aspect of this phase is to be completely realistic, but not overly pessimistic.

Keep in mind that one of the main purposes of this activity is for the innovator to learn enough about the other areas relevant to the iterative innovation process, in which she is not yet proficient, so as to become truly interdisciplinary. If you are a technology-oriented individual, this means that you want to pick up information and details about market needs, industry structure, the business models of your employer and other companies, etc. If you are a business-oriented person with some technical background to assist you, the objective is to understand details about the technology behind the products, the limits of the technology, and emerging technologies that may be better. Whatever the original domain experience, learning about the other elements of the iterative innovation process is essential. An indication that it is time to shift positions or companies is that your learning rate saturates.

From the perspective of the individual, existing companies in their real operating environments are going to play the largest role in the early part of the innovation process. Engagement with potential customers, regardless of whether they ultimately become customers, will be a cornerstone of early progress. Understanding the technology behind current products and services in the marketplace, and how they are evolving, and which ones are needed for the innovator's venture will be another cornerstone. And understanding industry structures and potential models for the company to achieve profitability in the most realistic way will be the third cornerstone. One cannot leave these issues to the future, especially given the absence of easy capital to finance later learning.

In the new innovation system, the individual innovator will have to access a variety of organizations to perform the iterative innovation process. She must engage, right from the start, customers and suppliers at companies in order to understand their markets, technology, business models, and industry structure. She must be aware of new potentially relevant knowledge at universities, so that her Technology arsenal is complete. She must engage corporations for potential support, be it payment for prototype development or in-kind support, and she must engage governments for appropriate project funding, such as through Small Business Innovation Research (SBIR) grants. And this process must take place globally, as supply chains and customers are spread across the globe. Given the small probabilities involved, finding the right organizations requires an initial large set of organizations to communicate with in order to zero in on appropriate partners, suppliers, customers, and technology sources.

With the process we described, the potential innovator takes charge of training herself through experiential learning and she will also generate her own innovation investment. She is thus self-sufficient, at least initially, and can innovate in the 3-to-10 year gap. De-risking the innovation during the early iterations on self-generated funds is most efficient since the investment decisions are always in synch with the iterative innovation process. Growing the business organically, with no outside equity investment, will of course be the best way to proceed — and the most profitable! But having de-risked the venture independently makes it also a most attractive investment opportunity for others, for now the innovator can educate investors about the risks based on quantifiable facts established through the iterative innovation process.

The fact that the Market and Implementation knowledge for many new growth areas will be global in nature presents an additional challenge to innovators. We must recognize that in the past, the U.S. was a great market for innovators from the U.S., but such a simple formula no longer holds. Smaller countries that have invested in moving quickly towards a knowledge-based economy, like Singapore with its five million citizens, have always faced the fact that all large markets lie outside the country. This required the innovator in Singapore to somehow hook into Market and Implementation information outside the country. In the new era, U.S. innovators will find themselves in a similar situation as these Singaporean innovators: many large high-growth markets are global, and therefore, the innovator will need to learn about global Markets and global Implementation in order to converge on fundamental innovations of value to large markets. This adds cross-cultural skills to the list of skills a successful innovator must possess. Even with international exposure during upbringing or education, international business is best learned in a corporate job that requires travel and transactions around the world.

In this new era, innovators who do a good job of self-schooling in the manner we've described will become highly valued beyond a single organization. The reasons have to do with trust and reliability. The financial crisis caused much broken trust. Lack of trust comes from lack of transparency about underlying asset values and risks. The default assumption has become that people or organizations deliberately misrepresent the "real" value of assets. For some people that you may talk to, the mistrust has gotten to the point where the farther the time horizon of the investments or ventures you are discussing, the more they will think you are underestimating the risk, and therefore the more they will overestimate it. In order for trust to return so that fundamental innovations can be supported properly over their long development cycles, the innovators in this new era must be able to present themselves as honest brokers of well-derived information. By understanding Market, Technology, and Implementation, the innovators who protect their own brand name will become the "Consumer Reports" evaluators of promising innovations in the pipeline. As trusted sources, they will be sought after during the years to come.

Reputable innovators who work honestly with corporations and investors are a necessary ingredient for building the new innovation pipeline over the next decade. The new innovation system needs to financially reward such innovators to maximize their impact and encourage them to help train the next generation. Others will observe that these innovators are in a lucrative position, which will produce more such innovators, eventually creating greater output of fundamental innovations.

Unfortunately, growing the pool of properly trained innovation talent is likely to be the main bottleneck in building a new innovation system, and this is compounded by three problems that reinforce each other. First, potential innovators can only determine their "fit" with the iterative innovation process by experiencing it first-hand, and they need to acquire the necessary cross-disciplinary skill set through experiential learning. The only practical way to accelerate and enhance the learning curve is through mentoring by experienced innovators while performing iterative innovation. Such training took place in the forward-looking corporate research laboratories, which continuously renewed this critical resource. Since the disappearance of those labs, the number of experienced innovators who could effectively help train new talent has constantly declined. Second, becoming an experienced innovator takes a relatively long time itself, due to the amount of skills and experiences that need to be accumulated in many areas. And third, many who have participated in start-up companies, company acquisitions, and/or universities have taught a whole generation of students that venture-capital-backed entrepreneurship in the age of inexpensive capital is the answer to growth and prosperity, while ignoring real innovation. This still-prevailing myth introduces another time lag, for such beliefs are slow to change. We want to highlight the reluctance to give up this belief with the following example.

One of the authors recently attended a conference on science and technologies that may produce innovations in 10 years or so. A potential innovator-entrepreneur approached, in order to receive insights from an experienced innovator-entrepreneur-scientist. Despite the burst of the financial bubble, this person was describing attempts that he had made to raise money for a new company that would supply equipment in a particular field. His interest was genuine in that he was asking about the process, what he should change, and so on. To be polite, advice was first offered on his entrepreneurial questions. Staying true to the reality of constrained capital and the reality of needing repeated iterations, advice was also offered on how he could advance the idea with some of his own funds in order to find a path which required less capital, and then approach the companies that he planned to sell to in order to receive funds for prototype development. Despite encouragement, one could tell that he yearned for the days of easy capital. He never asked about how to execute on the new recommended path, confirming that, deep down, he rejected the reality of this new era.

The importance of integrated Market-Technology-Implementation skills within the individual innovator was understood long before we formulated our iterative innovation model. As Vannevar Bush stated in 1942, the engineer "was not primarily a physicist, or a business man, or an inventor, but [someone] who could acquire some of the skills of each of these and be capable of successfully developing and applying new devices on a grand scale". The need now is for innovators who can cultivate these qualities, and more.

The years ahead are not for the faint of heart. But the new Intels, Microsofts and Apples need to be born, along with new difference-making and growth-generating ventures of all types and sizes. They will remain largely invisible during the time required to build them from the bottom up, as the era of raising large amounts of external capital in order to race to market, amid wide publicity, is over.

The Free Market Investor

Easy capital prior to the burst of the financial bubble allowed the early innovator to step back from realistically interacting with Market and Implementation. It provided incentives for premature entrepreneurship while ignoring the real innovation process, which in turn destroyed fundamental innovation efficiency. As we build a new innovation system, investors who are in synch with the iterative innovation process will benefit tremendously, while those who stick to the previous investment behaviors will be left behind.

Since most financiers are forced to operate at some level of abstraction, investment trends in certain sectors or certain investment models exert a strong force on the individual investor. It is hard to make decisions against a trend unless one has potent reality-based reasons to do so. Spotting the new trend and going along for the ride is much easier. These traits of financiers are well catered to as long as a paradigm keeps producing real investment opportunities. The information-age paradigm based on Moore's Law, with semiconductors, personal computers, cell phones, operating systems, application software, Internet hardware and web applications, created wave after wave of new and real investment opportunities. Towards the end of the paradigm, however, investors failed to adjust and started forcing their "proven" information-age investment models into other sectors, resulting in venture-capital-driven bubbles such as in the biotech or energy sectors.

Let's have a closer look at the energy sector for examining the difference between trend-driven investment behavior and investment decisions anchored in innovation reality. Early stage investors hoped that energy would be the same as the semiconductor-PC-IT sector, but alas it simply does not behave like that. The main reason is that unlike the semiconductor-PC-IT sector, energy does not have fundamental innovations driving many other layers of innovation. Other details matter, too, so let's review some of them.

First, a new form of energy will not be discovered. Humankind knows of all the forms, and the scale of the corresponding forces, so there will be no new form of energy analogous to the birth of the transistor or integrated circuit, which were completely new in multiple technical and economic dimensions. Second, the behaviors of energy sources and energy production are completely understood and established in the field of thermodynamics. So, new processes that change energy efficiency or the energy output of a device by orders of magnitude, as Moore's Law changed processing power by orders of magnitude, will not be discovered. Lastly, whereas the information-technology-related industries were themselves new in the last half of the twentieth century, the same is not true of the energy industries. People have been generating energy commercially, and producing the equipment and the infrastructure for it — for energy generated in power plants, in local installations, and in motorized vehicles — for well over a hundred years. The maturity of the main markets is revealed by energy being controlled by huge companies, conglomerates or nation-states. Thus, venture capital investments in energy inherently face a mature playing field in which entry barriers are enormously high. It is hard to imagine new venture-funded entrants gaining a substantial foothold and paying timely, home-run returns without fundamental innovation that offers very dramatic performance gains, such as by orders of magnitude — which is not possible without breaking the laws of thermodynamics.

Please note that this last statement is completely different from those examples of famous innovators being even more famously wrong about future markets, as in saying that no one would want a personal computer. Such predictions were incorrect in anticipating future consumer behavior. Breaking the laws of thermodynamics is a physical impossibility. Scientifically, the Moore's Law paradigm was the opposite case. Ever more transistors could be packed into tiny chips because as Gordon Moore, a chemist and physicist, understood, basic physical principles made it *possible*. Considering these details, it is amazing that any investors could have credibility by suggesting that investment in energy would be equivalent to previous investments in the information-age paradigm.

This is not to say that energy cannot be a good targeted investment. All sorts of profitable scenarios are possible, and we do not imply anything about the broader social and economic aspects of energy issues. The point is that returns on energy investments in general will be a far cry from the kind of returns that were possible from semiconductor-PC-IT investments during the 1970s to 2000.

The first thing for modern investors to recognize is that the investment window during the information age paradigm was highly unusual. Naturally, when an unusual period lasts for decades, we tend to think that this type of investing environment is normal. New paradigms will emerge, even if they are not as extraordinary as the one that rained benefits on early investors in the Bay Area. However, we are currently moving into a period in which the main need for investors is to be innovation-focused as opposed to technology-focused — that is, to be building portfolios on the basis of the "fundamental" value that innovation, done by good innovators, can deliver, rather than around particular types of technology. Many of the best investors who started in the 1960s and 1970s remained innovation-focused. It was their success that led to a venture capital industry largely structured for the unusual case of the Moore's Law paradigm. The venture industry then presumed itself to be "mature", whereas it had mainly just gotten locked into a formula that worked for the times. It has yet to become mature in the sense of making timely adjustments to changing times. As is true for any form of innovation financing, it must make the transition to an innovation-based investment vehicle to be successful in the future.

So what then is the "innovation investment model" going forward? We can state that very simply: *For an individual investment, the iterative innovation process for that particular innovation is the investment model.* Understanding the uncertainties across all three categories of Market, Technology and Implementation and iterating to reduce them until converging on the innovation is the essence of the innovation process. This means that continuous, comprehensive and honest risk assessment is embedded in the iterative innovation process, which is exactly what the investor needs to know. In other words, each iterative innovation process represents the inherently accurate financial risk model for the corresponding investment. At the early stages of fundamental innovation, the risk may be too high for the free-market investor, and his investment may need to wait until the innovation has been sufficiently de-risked through initial iterations. But as long as the investor follows the innovation process closely and can have an honest relationship with the innovators, then he or she can have risk transparency. Obviously, the risk is only as transparent to the investor as the degree to which he or she can resolve it in detail, which in turn depends on how well the investor is versed in iterative innovation. The proficient innovation investor will be able to clearly enunciate the previous innovation iterations and the Market-Technology-Implementation challenges still ahead for each investment at any point in time.

It is difficult to imagine an early stage investor being able to discern the iterative innovation process details without similar experiences and skills in Markets, Technology and Implementation as required of the individual innovator. Not many venture capitalists have this experience. From knowing hundreds of venture capitalists since the 1990s, we estimate that less than five percent have this experience today. So, just as for individual innovators, we identify the lack of trained innovation talent as the bottleneck for building a new innovation system. In fact, overcoming the false beliefs of a generation of venture investors, who associate the dot-com-type experience with successful investing as long as you can exit in time, might prove to be an even higher challenge in terms of innovation training. Considering these generational factors, excellent early stage investors will likely need to come from the new wave of innovators who emerge over the next decade. Some of these successful innovators will move into finance, just as innovators became the early investors in the information age paradigm.

The era we are currently in, prior to the emergence of a new defining paradigm, means that a sector-based portfolio investment strategy, such as for the biotech or energy sectors, will easily be outperformed by innovation-based investment portfolios that evaluate each individual investment on the merit of iterative innovation. Innovation portfolio companies will thus not share common technology or market traits, but they will be companies based on excellent execution of iterative innovation, that are in the process of converging on fairly fundamental innovations, and that incorporate an organic approach to business growth. The iterative innovation process is difficult enough so that these companies will likely be able to sustain their competitive advantages in the market for many years, and thus command high profitability and high returns for the investor. Such opportunities will also be invisible to investors not skilled in iterative innovation.

If we are assessing the current times correctly, then investments specialized to a new paradigm will do very well, but this new paradigm may take decades to arrive. Recognizing these specialized investment opportunities early through the lens of the iterative innovation process will become the decisive advantage for the astute innovation investor. Early recognition does not mean early investment. In fact, the innovation investor really wants to identify and accompany the innovation processes well ahead of the need for investment. Thus, a first quality judgment can be made before more resolution becomes available on whether or not an innovation process is likely to converge. For example, we do know that the fundamental innovations to watch are those pursued by researchers who use Market and Implementation knowledge to focus on researching the right problems. We also know that these fundamental innovations will take 10 to 15 years to enter the marketplace. This, of course, means that a significant gestation period between the "Aha moment" and the first potential investment in a particular innovation is warranted. For fundamental innovation opportunities, such gestation periods tend to be on the order of five years or so. Thus, by tracking proficient innovators and interacting with them in the 3-to-10 year innovation gap, fundamental advances can be identified. Regardless of the timing of particular innovation investments, this interaction extends free-market investor activity further into the gap, bringing additional Market and Implementation knowledge to innovators while providing optimal visibility for the investors. Please note that it is to the benefit of both innovators and investors for this forward-looking interaction to be profound and meaningful in the context of the innovation process, rather than just superficial networking.

We would like to finish this section on the note of hope and practicality. Despite the average lower returns ahead, spectacular returns will be achieved by those investors who have the ability to achieve great resolution on the iterative innovation process. A new breed of interdisciplinary talent — science-engineering-business-finance — has the capability of forming a new high-return investment community. Its activity will stimulate the new innovation system and thus increase the likelihood for getting the next paradigm under way.

The Corporation

Within most U.S. corporations today, innovative capacity has been largely devolved by the competitive global environment discussed previously. Companies jettisoned their forward-looking laboratories, outsourced their manufacturing and optimized their organizational structures, thus improving profitability by increasing operating efficiency. Organizational and managerial expertise was paramount, and spreadsheets were optimized. The model for corporations became the "Operational Corporation". But firms across all sectors have now reached the limits of value to be wrung from this cycle and it has become very hard to improve the bottom line further. Going forward, shareholders will preferentially buy stock in a particular company only because they believe that it can beat all of the other well-optimized, operationally efficient companies and deliver above-market returns. Corporations need organic top-line growth, and for that they need to innovate. But taking advantage of the new age will require capability that no longer resides in most corporations.

Will corporations build large-scale forward-looking laboratories again? Although entirely possible, the force opposing such a trend is global competition, the same force that doomed the forward-looking laboratories decades ago. Unless a company happens to be dominating an economic sector with something akin to a monopoly business model, the cost of truly integrated laboratories is too high and the yield on investment too low. A more plausible approach is available, which takes a bit of explaining.

There will always be good individual innovators emerging within the ranks, especially if growing numbers of people follow the path we recommended in the section to The Individual Innovator — working at a company, building the interdisciplinary knowledge and skills they need while nursing an innovative idea. Some of these innovators may leave to start new companies in the future, but only few such companies are likely to become direct competitors. The record suggests rather that corporations benefit from new entities started by former employees through forming complementary relationships as partners, customers, or suppliers. Whether the innovator creates a new business within the corporation or eventually as a separate entity, the corporation stands to benefit. But there is another, probably even more crucial role for such skilled innovators in corporations. And that is to interact with the external innovation pipeline on the company's behalf. These interactions need to be "innovation-based" going forward rather than "transaction-based" as they have been in the past.

Transaction-based interactions are the kinds that have been common in recent years: acquiring start-up companies that have developed a valuable innovation, or, at the other end of the spectrum, licensing university technologies. Neither is likely to produce organic growth for the corporation in the next decade. Start-up acquisitions present obvious difficulties. The corporation becomes a bidder for innovations opaquely buried in small companies controlled by middlemen. If the iterative innovation process is close to complete and the innovation is real, then the value of the innovation is clear to multiple bidders and the price will be set accordingly by competitive bidding. The middlemen have to be paid, and usually they have to be paid handsomely. This does not mean that such acquisitions could not be beneficial for some specific strategic purposes, but that has little to do with organic growth through innovation. On the other hand, if the iterative innovation process in the small company is not complete, then the corporation is essentially acting as an innovation investor, and all that was said in the previous section for the free-market investor applies.

So what about the other end of the spectrum, the licensing of university patents? There certainly has been much emphasis on university intellectual property in the past as corporations, investors, and others attempt to work with universities to increase the rate of innovations moving to the marketplace. It is important to realize that there is an incorrect assumption at play here. This assumption is that some sort of innovation bottleneck resides in the university at the exit point, and that lots of very valuable innovations are just waiting to be released. Exactly why this assumption is incorrect will become clear during our detailed discussion in the university section, in the next chapter. But we can suggest some pertinent thoughts to consider right now.

First, innumerable attempts have been made by third parties to license university intellectual property, by acting as a broker/clearing house for efficiently finding the right buyer. They failed because the transaction costs outweigh the returns. Second, publicly shared statistical data show that major institutions like MIT receive only tens of millions of dollars per year in licensing revenue, very much less than the funding for the research in the first place. If the universities that are the most intimately networked with surrounding commercial activity, and supposedly produce some of the most valuable intellectual property, cannot earn more than that, how much unreleased value can there be? Third, given the 10-to-15 year timeline for fundamental innovations, we suspect that net-present-value calculations will show that licensing university patents that are *not embedded in an ongoing iterative innovation process* have very little or no value to industry on average. The misplaced emphasis on acquiring university intellectual property exists mainly because it is one of the few things that non-innovators outside the university can recognize as a tangible item. When university-generated intellectual property *is part of an ongoing iterative innovation process*, then it can be a very important piece. But to understand and capture the real value, the interaction needs to be innovation-based — that is, grounded in seeing where the process stands, and the worth of what has been done so far, and what is likely to lie ahead.

What to do? The answer is that successful corporations will take on an innovation-investor mindset. They will judiciously invest in, and cultivate, innovations-in-progress both at small companies and at universities. And for various innovations, they will find the appropriate ways to either assimilate the innovations into their businesses, or partner in bringing them to market. As corporations begin to act as such investors, that which was outsourced largely to venture capitalists and Wall Street will come home. The corporation has several distinct home advantages:

- Intimate Market and Implementation knowledge of the corporation's current markets.

- Field expertise in Technology and Implementation.
- Access to cheaper capital than free-market investors (at least for the foreseeable future).
- And, coming back to those people within the ranks, ideally a cadre of skilled innovators who can efficiently interact with the new innovation pipeline.

The home disadvantages are:

- The "not invented here" syndrome among corporations that survived the era of bureaucratic capitalism: inherent resistance to taking such an approach.
- Reluctance to make the organization fit the innovation — and a tendency to instead force the innovation to fit the organization.
- Innovation absorption barriers due to lack of skill and knowledge at the interface with the new innovation pipeline.
- Reluctance to handle more than one unknown simultaneously (e.g. reluctance to enter a new market with a new technology).

Notice that all the home advantages are very real, while the disadvantages are mainly organizational or cultural limitations that can be overcome. Thus, the executive office will change in many corporations. The CEO will still need to be able to oversee operational efficiency, but the COO will be squarely tasked with running current cash cows as efficiently as possible. The CEO and CTO will have to lead the growth part of the corporation — as it will *not* be sufficient just to do "innovation investment" in some separate arm of the company, such as corporate venture funds. Certainly those venture funds could be seen as precursors of what we're talking about, in some ways. But we are talking about making innovation investment the central and integral part of the corporation. It will be the chief source of fundamental innovation and growth, while the operating side focuses on incremental innovation and near-term competitiveness (which is also essential work that demands expert attention).

Over the next few years, the corporation's market value will still be determined by the operational side. However, beyond that time horizon, the market value will be determined by the growth part of the company. Thus, in terms of the model that will *differentiate* a company, the Operational Corporation will fade into sunset while we see a concomitant rise of the Innovation Corporation.

The Innovation Corporation will concentrate on innovation with a 3-to-5 year time horizon, and will want some activity beyond that. To achieve this, it needs to engage new internal and external processes. Internally, corporations will have to recycle previous concepts that have had little success in the past, but can have traction in the new innovation pipeline. Internal incubators and internal investment schemes that include some means of external validation will evolve. Externally, corporations will need new interfaces to feed the internal processes, such as, for example, the Innovation Interface that specializes in bridging the industry-university innovation gap.

It is likely that the internal processes will be more focused on the later stage of the innovation process, whereas the external processes must be effective at starting or advancing the innovation process for medium-term and fundamental innovations outside the corporation. The workings of these external processes — addressing all the elements of iterative innovation, Market, Technology and Implementation — will draw the corporation into close involvement with other organizations across the entire spectrum of activity. The Innovation Corporation thus participates very actively in the new innovation system, as it contributes crucial knowledge to innovation processes that take place in the current 3-to-10 year gap.

The new Innovation Corporation will also be an astute purchaser of innovation, which means that sellers will have to produce higher-quality companies or technologies to sell. Thus, a more efficient marketplace for innovation will evolve outside the corporation, but it will be first necessary to have a sizable number of Innovation Corporations. Once enough are formed, however, other organizations such as investment groups and universities will have to improve their own roles to participate.

Corporations will obtain high growth by understanding their own new role in this system. A seat at the innovation table will allow them to tell the chef their favorite dishes; many of the entrees will be to their liking, and they may make new friends at the table as well. And with these benefits will come new responsibilities — more external partnering and funding to enhance the innovation flow all around the table.

Chapter 8

Building a New Innovation System:
The Research and Education Side

Individual innovators, free-market investors and corporations stand to benefit greatly from building a new innovation system, but their activities alone will not build it. Universities and governments must also embrace change and contribute actively. Nearly all fundamental and many medium-term innovations require research as a significant component. And by "significant" we mean not only the importance of the research, but the following.

Recall from our strained silicon example that iterative innovation took 13 years from the AT&T Bell Labs discovery to the first microprocessor with strained silicon being sold. But there were also five years of iteratively guided research leading up to the "Aha moment" at Bell Labs, and further research both at the Labs and at MIT afterward. The innovation was actually in research environments (first Cornell, then Bell Labs and MIT) for a total of 10 years, and the innovation was then completed over the next eight years through iterations in the market by the start-up AmberWave. Although timelines and transition points may vary with particular innovations and with changed conditions in the macro-environment, they will not be much different, since we have shown that 10 to 15 years between the Aha moment and first product sold is generic for fundamental innovations.

With the disappearance of basic research at corporate labs, universities and government laboratories are the only existing organizations that can perform the research required for fundamental innovations. As both are funded nearly exclusively by government for their research, we will not distinguish between them further in the following discussion and just refer to both as universities. We've shown that there have been great difficulties in connecting university activity to Market and Implementation, especially since the atrophy of the "scientific commons" as corporate labs withdrew from the scene. But we also know that Vannevar Bush's doctrine of publicly funding scientific research to create economic growth has worked well in many cases in the past. In fact, it worked so well that the majority of nation-states around the world have created similar university research funding programs. What can nation-states do that private investors cannot? It is important to understand research funding as an *investment*, not only to try and quantify the return to society, but to identify the optimum environment for yielding innovations.

Although it is very difficult to accurately quantify the return on investment (ROI) for nation-state funding of research, Lester Thurow made a comprehensive attempt in his book *Building Wealth: The New Rules for Individuals, Companies, and Nations in a Knowledge-Based Economy*. By aggregating and averaging various works at the time, he arrived at an approximate annual ROI of 66% for the United States. Regardless of what the exact number might be, this level of annual ROI is spectacular and certainly seems to justify Vannevar Bush's doctrine. Granted, Thurow's book was published in 1999, and since the data in it was drawn from previous years, it reflects the period of highest innovation productivity. But Thurow also showed that companies could not reach the same annual ROI on their own research investments at the time. How can that be? Why can a nation-state like the U.S. benefit so much from its research investments?

The answer lies in the size of the ecosystem or organization. Let us first note that the innovation process can only be completed in the free market, which takes probably somewhere between three and eight years depending on how fundamental the innovation is. The government invests in a huge research portfolio, generating a vast amount of new Technology options which could become relevant to innovations. But recall, from earlier discussions in this book that innovators also employ older and existing technologies in their innovations — including ones from research funded previously. Since the U.S. government invests in its research portfolio on behalf of society and for the benefit of society, all economic growth contributions from all innovations using its research become part of the government's ROI, no matter which organization ultimately brings an innovation to market and profits from it. It does not even matter which sector of the economy ultimately deploys the innovation. For example, if the government funds a medical Technology that eventually converges as an innovation in semiconductors 15 years later, the U.S. still benefits from the growth created by that innovation. It counts towards the national ROI, and rightly so. On the other hand, a medical equipment corporation would not benefit similarly if it had made the same research investment 15 years earlier. Its ROI on that investment is zero or near zero.

Because the government has no need to own innovations for commanding its ROI, absolutely anything that advances innovation is to its benefit, including organizational transitions, failures that others learn from, sharing of knowledge between researchers and corporations, etc. In other words, all innovation-relevant transactions that occur in the free market and in the research communities will contribute to the ROI of the government's research investment portfolio, whether or not these transactions benefit the actors who actually conduct them. We're going to continue the discussion, but what this means so far can be summed up pretty simply. While there is plenty of room for improving the efficiency of innovation that involves basic research, we must keep in mind that it is completely possible for a society to benefit financially if the system is large enough.

We can describe the relationship between nation-state research investment and innovation/economic growth more concisely using financial language. When the government invests in a broad "innovation market portfolio" on the research side, it benefits from diversifying "idiosyncratic innovation risk". The higher the "innovation market liquidity" — i.e. the easier it is for the innovation process to overcome transactional hurdles — the better the diversification of risk. Free market dynamics with open competition, low barriers to entrepreneurship, ease of organizational transformations, etc. increase "innovation market liquidity" on the free-market side. Exchange and accessibility of research results and scientific debate increase "innovation market liquidity" on the research side. Corporations, on the other hand, can only diversify their research portfolios to the extent that it is likely that they will be able to retain any resulting innovations and execute on them in the marketplace. The risk of not being able to capture a resulting innovation scales inversely with the breadth of company business and thus company size. Before leaving the portfolio investment analogy, we want to point out that "systemic innovation risk" or "undiversifiable innovation market risk" corresponds to the quality of our overall innovation system.

Pondering the research investment model allows us to understand why nation-states are likely to be the investors in early stages of fundamental innovation but corporations will not be. It also explains why corporations decisively cut forward-looking research laboratories when they faced more competition, and why it was possible for monopolies or sector-dominant companies to support such laboratories. A monopoly has guaranteed revenue, fairly independent of normal business factors. It also benefits from any innovation in the economic sector it dominates, unless it blocks commercialization because of organizational barriers that such large corporations tend to generate internally. As was seen in the large vertically integrated corporations during the end of the bureaucratic capitalism era, the inability of monopolies to complete iterative innovation on the market side is very pronounced. Thus, high "innovation market liquidity" based on free market dynamics must be a core attribute for any successful innovation system in a globally competitive environment.

There are interesting consequences to understanding this model, especially with respect to how the "free market side" and the "research and education side" of the innovation system fundamentally relate to each other. We can highlight the interdependence with these juxtaposed statements:

- Free market ROI must rely on the nation-state to invest in the early iterations of fundamental innovation, because free market actors cannot do so profitably by themselves.
- Nation-state ROI must rely on the free market to competitively finish the later iterations of fundamental innovation, because the nation-state cannot realize its profits otherwise.

Other than the case of monopolies or sector-dominant companies (the only meta-stable in-between possibility), it is interesting to see so clearly how the two sides of the innovation system are necessarily co-dependent. With a clear understanding of the iterative innovation process and its implications, many long-standing ideological battles in macroeconomics seem rather pointless.

The 3-to-10 year innovation gap appears as a natural consequence of the innovation investment model. As discussed in the previous sections, free-market investors and corporations will benefit greatly from reaching into the innovation gap as they will compete for innovation opportunities. With the right innovation expertise they will be able to determine the right timing for investments, but they will not be able to reach all the way across the gap. As a consequence, a "valley of death" exists between early fundamental innovation funding and the time when private capital will be invested. Before we address the resources that the government can provide for crossing the valley, we must note that there is a positive feature of this valley. Since the resources are so scarce at this point of the iterative innovation process, it is up to the innovator to bring the innovation across. His or her ingenuity in de-risking the potential innovation further and his or her use of personal funds, which often involves hard decisions affecting one's personal life, effectively act as a filter for both the quality of the innovation and the quality of the innovator. Technology that was not iterated properly through Market and Implementation early, and less promising innovations in general, will and should fail to cross this financial void. Too much funding, as during the venture capital bubbles (fueled by very low cost capital in the economy), will bring across too many ideas that should have been filtered. On the other hand, when financial conservatism dominates, the valley can be too deep, not allowing even the most promising innovations and the best innovators to cross.

As for mechanisms available for crossing the valley: beyond methods such as the use of personal funds, and early partnering with potential customers or suppliers for prototype development or in-kind support, Small Business Innovation Research (SBIR) grants have been a very important mechanism in the U.S. SBIR funding is unique in that it is neither conventional research funding nor private capital. The sizes of the grants are substantial but not lavish, and they've proven to be very effective for iterating fundamental innovations across the gap in cases where neither out-of-pocket funding nor partnering help would have been enough. Also, organizations like the Department of Defense (DoD) behave as early adopters, helping innovations to cross the gap with longer-term strategic investments for the purpose of buying the innovative products.

Let's consider a historic example to show how important the government's role can be for fundamental innovation beyond the university research investment timeframe. In this case, the government acted through DoD as an early customer for the innovation, which turned out to be truly dual-use for defense and commercial applications. However, the government must carefully guard against its role in the innovation gap so as not to distort the Market for the innovators by introducing unintended subsidies. Such Market distortions can cause the innovations to converge differently, or can allow them to exist only as long as the government support remains in place. We shall pick up on this fine line again in the Government section.

Since the semiconductor industry responsible for Moore's Law and the information age paradigm evolved largely in the free market, few are aware of the important role that DoD played during the birth of the industry. We've described how William Shockley, one of the inventors of the transistor, left AT&T Bell Labs, where the "fundamental innovation research" on the transistor was performed. Let us now re-trace the rest of the story while adding in an angle not mentioned before. A few years after leaving Bell Labs, the inventor formed the Shockley Semiconductor Laboratory within an electronics company in Palo Alto, California. His intent was to commercialize silicon transistors. Why did he continue the innovation iterations with silicon, when *germanium* was used as the material in the early Bell Labs transistors? Because DoD wanted higher power transistors, and was going to invest through research contracts in this early and important work for its mission. Robert Noyce and seven others then left Shockley to form Fairchild Semiconductor — a division of an existing firm, Fairchild Camera and Instrument, which was already a significant defense contractor — where they indeed produced silicon transistors for military R&D and procurement contracts. Moreover, after the threat of Sputnik, small circuits were required for satellites. They needed to be small and weigh little for launching them into space. Fairchild was awarded research contracts to develop what became integrated circuits.

Once that innovation was well iterated, we know the rest of the story. Noyce and Gordon Moore left to form Intel, which became the leading and iconic manufacturer of integrated circuits. Along with other chipmakers, it triggered the economic growth of the information age. Moore's Law took over.

The highest growth sector of the worldwide economy over the last decades was thus enabled by U.S. government funding of early innovation iteration over the course of many years, through the Department of Defense acting as an early customer. Nevertheless, private investors ultimately reaped large returns from Intel, Microsoft, Oracle, and a host of other new firms and subsequent innovations. As expected from our understanding of the iterative innovation process and the corresponding investment model, a detailed look at the origin of fundamental innovations, such as the integrated circuit, does not support a completely free-market innovation investment model.

During a pre-paradigm phase such as the one in which we find ourselves currently, private capital tends to be expensive. Well-selected and well-timed longer-term innovation investments by the government, especially when acting as a customer, can decrease the time required for starting the next paradigm. At the end of a paradigm, capital production outpaces the generation of new innovation opportunities, with all the destructive effects on the innovation system discussed previously, eventually leading to apparent stagnation. However, the cycle can be re-started as long as we actively build a new innovation system that will lead to the emergence of the next paradigm, with corresponding super-growth.

We'll say more about the role of government in our new era at the end of the chapter. Since universities have barely been brought into the discussion, let us now address them fully. This will take two subsections: on the research mission, and on the education mission, of universities in the context of building a new innovation system. The fact that the research subsection is longer has nothing to do with relative importance. The state of university research today involves a number of factors that the non-academic reader may not be very familiar with, so they need explaining, whereas for education we can draw upon insights developed earlier in the book about the skills and knowledge required for iterative innovation.

Universities: The Research Mission

The new innovation system will require universities to re-evaluate both their perceived role and real role in the innovation process. To recap briefly: for many years in the postwar era, the university's role was to provide research, and research talent, for a system in which the corporate labs performed fundamental innovation and were active in maintaining the scientific commons. With the erosion of the corporate labs and the commons came the shift. The universities became nearly the sole providers of basic research, *and* were either perceived as driving or were expected to drive practical, fundamental innovation — without anything near the previous measure of guiding signals, interaction and support from the dwindling corporate innovation system.

This continues to be the universities' situation. Imagine being the president of a university thrust into accepting a role at the center of the innovation system. Companies are asking the universities for well-developed innovations that they need for growing their businesses; venture capitalists are trolling the halls in search of the same for investment in start-ups. You do not have those well-developed innovations; you mainly have pieces of research Technology and a lack of Market and Implementation capabilities for producing actual innovations. But a number of people are trying to commercialize the technologies anyway, and meanwhile the public officials of your local region are perhaps wondering why the university's start-ups aren't generating the phenomenal growth expected. At the same time the federal government is asking for real-world metrics that show return for its funding of basic research; alumni are asking for more start-ups and innovations which they can either participate in or boast about; and students are expecting the university to train them to enter an open innovation world, fully equipped with all the skills for rapid success.

Since not many of your research technologies are scoring decisive wins in the marketplace, your revenues from licensing the technologies are low. Perhaps the latest proposed fix to the tech-transfer office will remedy that, or perhaps the home-run technology that produces the world's next great start-up is just around the corner. At any rate, your faculty will always remind you that one goal is important above all: to keep the research funds flowing in.

This bizarre world is removed by at least one degree of separation, and probably more, from the realities of innovation. One encouraging sign is that people manage to get useful things done within this environment, sub-optimal though it may be. A closer look will show how truly out-of-touch the situation has become, and suggest ways of re-thinking the university's role so as to contribute more consistently and effectively to real innovation.

Most universities raise research funding today around any ideas that the government can be convinced to pursue. This in itself subtly distorts the nature of the relationship, transforming the research universities from performers of a vital service to a special interest group seeking support for its latest cause. Without the forward-looking corporate labs, and without many other good connections to true Market needs and Implementation realities, basic scientific research is generated in a government-university loop of non-reality that lacks feedback from the world of real applications. It is not surprising that the iterative innovation process cannot proceed in universities alone, and that random scientific knowledge is created as opposed to critical basic scientific knowledge in areas both needed and feasible for application. There is no proper mechanism for guidance on a crucial issue: what would be most useful for researchers to be researching in the first place. And whereas constant, iterative reality-checking can steer research in a direction that would really lead to fundamental innovation — or shut it off, if it isn't headed that way — the approach now used allows research to go off upon long and fruitless tangents.

To illustrate the difference between "fundamental innovation research", which employs the early iterative innovation process to formulate the right research questions, and "random scientific research", which generates research questions based on the funding that can be obtained, let's look at a direct comparison of how a specific research topic played out in AT&T Bell Labs versus the university environment.

This case shows Bell Labs to have been much more efficient in filtering innovative concepts than universities. It involves the response of these two environments to advances in carbon-based materials. In the so-called "closed innovation" environment of Bell Labs, in the later years of its functioning as a basic-research hub, the existence of a cage-shaped carbon molecular structure called a Buckyball fascinated scientists and captured their attention. As was typical with a new hot area, a team formed within the Labs that was interested in this area, and started contributing to research knowledge. Initially, much effort was expended on just understanding this science and technology area, since little was known. But an emphasis on the material's functional properties was soon established. Why? Only when the properties were known could iterative innovation start. One needs to know what the material can do differently from other materials, in order to start thinking about its usefulness for real applications. Thus, iterative innovation was started as soon as possible.

After three to four years or so, it became clear from iteration that considering all factors, it was unlikely there would be an innovation convergence. Although Buckyballs were very interesting, it did not make sense to invest in them further. Research groups were told to move on to other areas with greater potential. Today, almost 20 years later, there are no major innovations in the marketplace employing Buckyballs.

This entire process occurred within the walls of AT&T, and a similar process occurred within the walls of other corporate laboratories. Information was shared at a scientific level with the outside so that other stakeholders in the innovation ecosystem could also determine the potential of the research area. Bell Labs was a fairly optimized environment for early fundamental innovation iteration. When an innovation opportunity emerged from Bell Labs, anybody who desired to take on subsequent iterations, whether within AT&T or not, could evaluate risk knowing that Bell Labs had performed "fundamental innovation research" diligently. The first part of the innovation process had been performed by a trusted source able to gauge the prospects for real value.

While Bell Labs research into Buckyballs lasted only a few years during the early 1990s before it was determined that innovation convergence would not occur, an almost identical interest in carbon materials appeared in the university environment, which lasts until today. Another type of molecular carbon structure called a carbon nanotube became the rage. The nanotube's structure is in some ways very similar to the Buckyball (they're both called "fullerenes"), but in a cylindrical shape instead. Immediately, legions of academic researchers drew pictures involving nanotubes inserted in almost every application imaginable. These researchers persuaded many government funding agencies that since the area was very hot and had presumably many applications, large funding was needed. Universities lined up, and a large amount of research grants were given to many universities in parallel for pursuing carbon nanotubes.

A literature search in 2010 returned over 50,000 publications on carbon nanotubes, and almost every scientific conference over the past decade has been filled with random scientific knowledge on this topic. What is even more startling is that the number of publications on carbon nanotubes has been significantly increasing every year, for the past 18 years, with no maximum reached as of the end of 2009. Journals and science periodicals have oriented themselves to this new open-innovation age and become the *People* magazines of the science world, publishing the latest fads and cartoons exciting imagination about nantotubes — with their impact soon to come! The outside world cannot distinguish between this "coming of age" of nanotubes and the previous age in which organizations of experience, like Bell Labs, filtered by performing early fundamental innovation iteration correctly.

Moreover, many start-up companies were formed on the basis of nanotube technology and the venture capital model forced them to pursue the path of commercialization, despite the fact that they were slowly realizing it was probably a bad idea that should have been killed early. As of 2010, carbon nanotubes had not significantly impacted any product, despite the 18 years of investigation. Much investment went in early, without any proper innovation iteration. The future of nanotubes is likely to be the same as Buckyballs. Interesting curiosities, but they are not an advantage in any market yet known.

Note that both ecosystems produced basic knowledge about a new carbon-based material that could hypothetically be used in the future for various innovations, the key word being hypothetically. There is certainly value in understanding these materials and making sure that their unusual characteristics, which are many, are properly documented in papers or patents. But random scientific research is highly inefficient, for it allows true iterative innovation to start only much later, after much redundant research money has been spent and often companies have been formed and failed prematurely. For "fundamental innovation research", on the other hand, the researcher applies innovation metrics from the very start and thus has a very different purpose than a researcher who chooses a research problem based on funding opportunities and his or her curiosity and self-interest.

This is not to say that we assign zero value to research that is pursued for the sake of adding knowledge in areas that appear to have no connection to useful applications, or that keeps being pursued beyond the point when usefulness for applications appears highly unlikely. This type of research falls into a category of expenditure similar to art. The original product of the endeavor, whether it is a research finding or a work of art, is considered useful and valuable in itself, albeit for varying reasons. But we must separate this type of research from fundamental innovation research due to the different investment models and investment goals. Government funders can then invest in two categories: fundamental innovation, for the ultimate goal of economic growth (with a lot of this type, since that is what the public expects), and research that is expanding knowledge in areas of interest to society but likely not connected to economic growth (with a little of this type). Although difficult to quantify, our experience points to a large imbalance currently: most of society believes it is funding research that will spur innovation and economic growth, but most research activity lies closer to the random research type.

Fundamental innovation research is difficult to seed in most universities, as it requires some knowledge of real Markets and Implementation. In very technology-oriented universities, some fraction of faculty members spend a significant amount of their time interacting with Market and Implementation outside the university in order to pursue fundamental innovation research, but this fraction is typically small and depends on personal initiative. The individuals who pursue Market and Implementation knowledge are typically not rewarded for such activity in academe, due to the uncomfortable nature of the interface between the university and the outside world. The fundamental innovation research interests of professors often stem from their early careers in the now-extinct corporate research laboratories, and are thus a remnant of our past innovation ecosystem, not exactly a non-renewable resource but one hard to renew. A major challenge in trying to encourage more fundamental innovation research, as opposed to "random scientific research", is a shortage of real innovators in university and government leadership positions. Yet getting this balance corrected is a critical aspect of repairing our innovation system.

To elucidate the challenge, let us imagine the new assistant professor joining a research university today. The former corporate research labs are no longer a source for new professor hires. Thus, most junior professors are very green, either being employed from graduate school or after a short stint as a post-doctoral associate at another academic institution. This new professor may have an interest in commercialization and even dream of launching a start-up, but how is he going to perform iterative innovation? How can he focus on *the right research problem*, when he has had no Market or Implementation exposure that would allow him to efficiently annihilate potentially non-innovative paths early on?

The young professor also has another pressing concern demanding his attention. To earn academic tenure he should accumulate significant research publications, and he will be judged as well by his ability to draw research funds. He must survive by finding a "visible research area" and being funded to do work in it. By satisfying these goals the professor has a much higher chance of staying and rising in the university. In the past, as we have learned, the iterative innovation processes in corporate labs mostly defined the "visible research areas". Today these areas are created synergistically, through a self-assembled process of many professors with similar goals, and government officials forced to allocate basic research dollars. The process has created a plethora of long-running programs, funded with tens of millions of dollars, that could have been killed at an early stage by the first iteration of Technology-Market-Implementation sketched out on the back of an envelope. A signature of this problem is that many of the research areas produce output that later encounters Market and Implementation barriers that are infinitely tall. Such tremendous incompatibilities can be known up front. However, the process that would reveal them is replaced with cartoons and comic-book sketches envisioning science fiction that is not questioned in the peer-dependent funding mechanisms, which are no longer balanced by the participation of corporate researchers who have basic-research skills *and* experience with Market and Implementation.

What is a university to do with respect to its research mission? The principal choice is between focusing on random scientific investigations more or less by default, as at present, and focusing on innovation and innovation processes, which means active change and participation in building our new innovation system. Note that the latter choice can potentially be made while keeping the same sort of university departments as we have today. But once the choice is made, how can a system transformation be seeded, to move in the chosen direction?

We doubt that there is a single easy answer, but believe that a combination of approaches can seed the system change. A good starting point for thinking about possible approaches seems to be the three principal "nutrients" required for the iterative innovation process we listed earlier. To sum them up, the requirements are:

- skilled innovation talent,
- appropriate innovation investment,
- and an environment that allows innovators to focus on the iterative innovation process.

We have just seen that hiring new professors who are already trained in innovation is not much of an option any longer as the talent pool has dried up. However, the university does have control over the tenure process. We are not necessarily suggesting any radical changes to the process itself, but changing some of the criteria and their weighting could be highly effective. To start with, emphasis could be placed during the hiring of new faculty on their desire and intent to perform "fundamental innovation research", and their willingness to actively engage in the experiential learning processes. For example, a candidate for a position in which fundamental innovation research is to be performed should display an appropriate interest in interacting with Market and Implementation. As most universities have some senior faculty members with proven innovation track records, they could be more prominently involved with evaluating the intentions and potentials of new hires vis-à-vis becoming an innovator. They could also act as mentors during the tenure process and support research faculty in acquiring Market and Implementation skills. Steps actively taken towards building innovation skills, like meaningful interactions with industry, should be rewarded. Progress in applying Market and Implementation knowledge to research problem formulation could be included in tenure evaluation criteria. De-emphasizing journal articles on random scientific research while emphasizing progress on real innovation processes, whether it results in a journal article or not, would significantly contribute to shifting the current balance.

Moreover, new professor hiring could stipulate industry experience in Market or Implementation instead of the currently required academic continuity. Would a candidate with excellent PhD research and a few years in a non-research industry position really make a worse professor than one who boosted his publication list with random scientific research over the same period as a post-doctoral associate? We believe that universities can do much on the personnel side to shift incentives towards enabling more innovation talent.

Shifting research *investment* is more difficult for universities because they have less direct influence. In principle, universities have three funding sources: government, industry, and self-generated funds, the latter primarily from endowments. We will leave the discussion of potential ways to steer government investments towards more fundamental innovation research to the subsequent Government section. Funding from industry would of course be good in the sense that it would bring with it the much needed Market and Implementation context, but research investment with a timeline at the far end of the 3-to-10 year gap is not affordable for individual companies. It would of course be self-defeating if universities were to cross the gap completely and take short-term corporate funding to perform outsourced development work. Such a strategy is as dangerous and ineffective as obtaining research funding for ideas born in a vacuum. There is, however, one promising form of industry research investment, albeit usually meta-stable and difficult to sustain.

That form of research investment can come from industry-university consortia, partially funded by government. A consortium can take on longer-term research leading to a fundamental innovation, and contribute knowledge of Market and Implementation as well. An example of fairly successful effort is the MARCO consortium program created by the Semiconductor Research Corporation (SRC). Research is funded in broad areas anticipated to be of future value to the industry, and the work is carried out in universities. Multiple top universities are involved, and industry guides the research with company representatives, largely through periodic conferences and reviews. In principle, such consortia have been excellent at creating an environment for early fundamental innovation iteration. But keep in mind that most of these programs were created during the information age paradigm governed by Moore's Law, and they still ride the coat-tails of this paradigm. This means that the Market and Implementation contexts for the consortia's fundamental innovation iterations are still the markets, business models, manufacturing implementations etc. of the current paradigm. Thus, the model works best when an industry is progressing in the heart of a paradigm, but will have difficulty at the end of a paradigm.

More importantly, however, market forces tend to work against consortia. Assuming a new fundamental innovation funded by the consortium somehow crosses the innovation gap sufficiently to reach the investment horizon of the corporations, it is then to the advantage of each corporation to try to exclusively capture that fundamental innovation and not share it with the other members of the consortium. Although we know that crossing sufficiently into the innovation gap purely from the university side is currently unlikely, the consortium members must assume it possible because otherwise they would not participate. If either this belief is undermined or the competitive forces are activated, then consortia will disintegrate. This, in turn, is the reason they tend not to be stable outside the heart of a paradigm.

The other theoretically conceivable non-government investment source for fundamental innovation research would be self-generated. Apart from the setbacks during the financial crisis, university endowments have grown and endowment interest is a growing fraction of the university operating budget. Endowed universities could thus become independently-funded foundations in the future. In such a case, the endowment interest could potentially dominate the institution's directions in research and education and move government research funding into a secondary role. More financially independent, the university could find it easier to implement policies and practices that encourage a focus on iterative innovation. However, considering the breadth of university activities, it would probably not be an easy task to align all interests behind self-funded "fundamental innovation research".

Finally, let's consider the third innovation nutrient: the innovation environment that allows innovators to focus on the iterative innovation process. What constitutes a good environment for early innovation iteration? We recall that the lower the transactional barriers for iterative innovation, the better. Universities are excellent at keeping the barriers for intellectual and technological transactions low, and provide the best access to knowledge resources through their libraries and similar infrastructures. They are also excellent at encouraging and protecting individual freedom. These environmental factors have been optimized for performing research in the past, and they are a requirement for performing fundamental innovation research today. In fact, they are also essential to innovation iterations in the 3-10 year innovation gap, which is why universities have an important infrastructural support role to play for advancing innovations beyond the research funding boundary line.

Overshadowing the excellent environment for Technology is the absence of real Market and Implementation knowledge, without which iterative innovation and thus "fundamental innovation research" cannot be performed. As mentioned earlier, the organizational barriers for interfacing with the outside world are high and they are currently only overcome by individual professors based on their personal initiative.

Recognizing that change in a dynamic economy usually occurs through the creation of new organizations, the authors of this book have worked over the past five years to evolve a new organization that could facilitate fundamental innovation processes in conjunction with universities, companies, and governments. Originally seeded at Cornell University, and mentioned earlier in this book, the Innovation Interface is now a not-for-profit educational entity that can be scaled to involve multiple universities. The current model involves students, faculty and companies in performing iterative innovation together in the 3-to-10 year gap. The work is organized into so-called Innovation Projects that nominally last one year and can be shaped and extended as needed. The Innovation Interface has so far focused on engaging corporations directly with Innovation Projects while training the next generation of innovators in the universities. We will describe the educational component of this integrated approach in more detail in the next section.

For the current discussion on the university innovation environment, we would like to share our experience that it is possible with this approach to sustainably innovate in the 3-to-10 year gap while bringing significant value to both corporations and universities. The direct involvement of corporations creates a Market and Implementation context that will not only have an influence on future research problem formulations of participating professors and students, but also on those of colleagues they interact with. Beyond the performance of the actual innovation processes, Innovation Projects thus provide a broader Market and Implementation context on campus. As we would expect, achieving stability in the innovation gap is not easy. Naturally, it requires the highest level of performance on iterative innovation. The dedication to the iterative innovation process enables the Innovation Interface to combine and integrate critical elements of the innovation environments on both sides of the gap, making it a unique place in the innovation gap for innovating and training innovators. The ability to contribute Market and Implementation components to universities should enhance the performance of fundamental innovation research.

Universities: The Education Mission

Today's lack of skilled innovators, along with the delays inherent in training the next generation, will likely present the rate-limiting factor for building a new innovation system. We need trained innovators at every stage of the innovation pipeline for performing iterative innovation as well as for investing in iterative innovation. We need them in universities to perform fundamental innovation research, we need them in the innovation gap to keep iterating through Technology, Market and Implementation while fighting the odds to survive, we need them in corporations to innovate in-house and to work externally with other innovators, and we need them to start companies. We also need them in government to invest skillfully on behalf of society. We need them in programs and organizations like SBIR and DoD that can help innovations across the "valley of death"; we also need them in corporate executive offices as the new CTOs and CEOs of the Innovation Corporation to invest for high organic corporate growth, and we need them to be the champions among the free-market investors who will seed the new super-growth companies of the future. So what role can universities play in training our next generation of innovators?

The wisdom that education is not so much about imparting knowledge as providing the opportunity for self-development is nowhere more true than for innovation education. Traditional education that relies on the standard combination of canned lectures, textbooks and problem sets or case studies will not produce students with an understanding of innovation and other interdisciplinary activities. Although it is likely that this traditional education model will be generally disrupted and gradually displaced, because it no longer meets today's market needs and can easily be replaced with cheaper versions employing modern communication technology, it is equally likely that not all universities will be innovative enough to move away from this education model. However, with a multi-stage interactive approach tailored to innovation education needs, universities can become powerful catalysts for accelerating the building of a new innovation system.

As we know from the now-extinct forward-looking corporate labs that trained many past and current innovators, the only really effective way to train an innovator is through mentorship while innovating. The core skills we derived in the earlier chapter "One Person, One Iteration at a Time" were (a) a high capacity for interdisciplinary learning, (b) the ability to abstract efficiently and correctly, (c) the ability to switch quickly between a bird's-eye view for seeing connections and ground-level detail for being right about the facts, and (d) the ability to make high quality decisions in the face of multiple uncertainties. Experiential learning is the only way to acquire this complex skill set across Technology, Market and Implementation, and learning while performing the iterative innovation process provides the failures and successes that ultimately build skill. Please note that it is the failures with subsequent corrections, preferably a large number of very small failures, that makes the iterative innovation process converge. A high level of self-criticism in the details, while maintaining overall confidence and resilience, is most important for making the many failure-correction loops quick and efficient.

Going through iterative innovation the first time is psychologically very challenging, and a young innovator encounters many points of near-despair when the way forward just does not want to become clear (which is ultimately compensated by the great feeling when it does). The role of the experienced innovator as a mentor becomes crucial in those moments for instilling confidence, suggesting different approaches or places to look, or helping out with some complementary pieces that are not yet within the grasp of the young innovator. The mentor probably doesn't know the particular answer either at this point. But having been there many times before, the mentor knows it can be figured out in one way or another, which is the reassurance the young innovator needs. Ultimately, the successful young innovator accumulates enough such experiences, building both confidence and innovation skills for self-sufficiency in iterative innovation.

At least some part of innovation mentorship needs to be provided during university education. But before examining how we can address this, we want to highlight another important function we have lost with the forward-looking corporate laboratories. University graduates who aspired to become innovators in the past actually had places to go to. The hand-off point between universities and corporate labs at the time was a student trained in basic research, but with little exposure to innovation. However, graduates knew they had an innovation support structure in the corporate lab environments to look forward to. Today, the situation for innovative students is worse both before and after graduation. Students involved in research programs that arise from the university-government non-reality loop are left with a distorted and incorrect idea of what research, innovation, and scientific productivity are. Graduates have learned the self-assembly game of raising government funds, and satisfying the subsequent research contracts with unimportant milestones. In such a process, we train the next generation of professors who efficiently coordinate as a special interest group. But what about the students who understand this and don't want go in this direction? Where do they go? This is the most prevalent unanswered questions among PhD students who want to innovate.

We have outlined a difficult but feasible path in the previous section on The Individual Innovator. However, we started with the assumption that our young innovator had at least figured out that becoming an innovator is what she should be doing based on some confidence that she could be good at it. But how can she have figured that out if she was never exposed to the real innovation process before? How could she know that she needs to iterate through Technology, Market and Implementation when all she heard was entrepreneurship stories that took place during the bubbles? The self-responsible path outlined in The Individual Innovator is feasible and it will be very profitable for the innovators who can succeed on it. But they certainly have to start with an enormous handicap today, because they basically have to make it all on their own with no preparation. How can we fix this crippling disconnect?

Since we are currently burdened with a lack of trained innovators who can effectively help teach and ultimately mentor our next generation talent, it is worthwhile to think about what an innovation education pipeline could look like under these constrained resource conditions. We need to recognize that not everybody can become an innovator. Talent comes in many shapes and forms, and with different preferences. Although we have gained some insights into common traits of innovators and innovation talent, the best and only sure way to find out is through self-selection when exposed to the iterative processes for fundamental and medium-term innovation. What does the innovation process feel like? When faced with the multiplicities, non-linearity and uncertainties of iterative innovation, students ultimately find it either uncomfortable or exhilarating. That is quite natural, as people have different comfort levels with being "outside the box", and they also have different kinds of outside-the-box thinking they enjoy or are good at. A creative design engineer may be good at that kind but not care about the others; a skilled on-the-spot negotiator or manager likewise. Yet becoming an innovator is all about choosing a life outside the box, and not just one aspect of it. As we've seen, iterative innovation continuously requires the innovator to make a deliberate and self-actuated move out of the box whenever the need or opportunity may materialize, in any fashion, because otherwise sequential risk reduction is not possible. Although some care is warranted not to overwhelm students completely upon first encounter, this perpetual embracing of uncertainty should not be disguised, because it is one of the most important self-selection criteria for students. So what should be the anatomy of an innovation education pipeline? One way to approach it is like a pyramid of self-selection and self-motivated engagement. Each level requires increased dedication from the student, but at each level the student also receives more dedicated innovation mentorship. This can principally be consistent with the aforementioned shortage of innovation mentors. For the sake of this discussion, let's consider four practical levels: General, Class Project, Innovation Project and Fundamental Innovation Research.

General exposure to the reality of the iterative innovation process could take on a similar form as entrepreneurship education during the past decade. Entrepreneurship was incorporated in courses and curricula across many disciplines, and spread successfully across campuses with seminars, clubs, celebrations, etc. Unfortunately, entrepreneurship without real innovation was overemphasized in courses, in response to stimulus from the investment community at the time, leaving the misguided impression among students that listening to bubble-time start-up stories would teach them what they need to know. Since it is of paramount importance to correct this myth anyway, and since the entrepreneurship networks on campuses generally have such good reach, it makes sense to introduce iterative innovation to a large student audience via this route and start balancing entrepreneurship with the real driver of economic growth, innovation. If we could generate a realistic appreciation for iterative innovation similar to the enthusiasm for entrepreneurship during the bubble times, we will have put an important piece for our new innovation system in place.

It also makes sense to have as many students as possible develop an appreciation for iterative innovation, no matter what they want to do later in their careers. Since a healthy innovation system is at the root of all our well-being, there exists a natural alignment of interest for society to support building our new innovation system. Popular support can only help our difficult task ahead. Understanding the iterative innovation process, what's involved in performing it and the roles of the stakeholders contributing to our innovation system avoids unrealistic expectations and enables communication about opportunities. We believe that everybody can contribute at some point to building our new innovation system, be it by performing incremental innovations as in the example of our restaurant owner, by interacting with the innovation system in professional roles as accountants, lawyers, or public officials, or by encouraging the kid next door in her aspirations to create that "next new big thing" that changes the world.

Class Projects can provide students with a first touch-and-feel experience of iterative innovation for determining how well they resonate with it. There are already a number of courses at various universities built around having students perform innovation projects for real-world "clients". The possible scope of these class projects tends to be confined by fitting the academic boundary conditions, such as a need for completion in one semester. However a good set-up within these constraints can provide students with a solid basis for their decisions. Based on our experience, in order to gain real innovation learning students need, at a minimum:

- One full iteration through Technology, Market and Implementation, with significant uncertainty in all three areas — not just Technology iteration, as may be the case in projects that focus on having teams of students build something that works.
- Quantitative analyses in both technical and business dimensions.
- At least the time of one semester for achieving sufficient depth.

Students are taught tools for their quantitative evaluations as they progress and their performance receives periodic critique and feedback from trained innovators. Despite limitation in scope, such class projects can help students figure out whether or not iterative innovation is for them and whether they should take the next steps.

Beyond class projects, innovation training needs to be embedded in 100% full and real innovation processes.

Innovation Projects are the new format of performing iterative innovation in the gap used by the Innovation Interface.

Fundamental Innovation Research is a PhD student's thesis research, if and only if the research problem has been defined by early iterations through Technology, Market and Implementation and he is mentored accordingly.

These last two formats of innovation training are very different but highly complementary. From the student's point of view, Fundamental Innovation Research starts with choosing a thesis research problem that results from early innovation iteration either as defined by his advisor or as he defines it himself. The latter is difficult because he has no research experience yet that would help him with defining a cutting edge research problem, nor does he have the Market and Implementation knowledge to help him with early iteration. He also will need project funding, which can sometimes be aided by fellowships. Since he will most likely rely on his advisor initially for thesis topic definition, he needs to choose an experienced innovator as his advisor. Hopefully, early exposure to the iterative innovation process as discussed above will enable him to do so. Iteration cycles during fundamental innovation research tend to be long with most time and money spent, not surprisingly, on Technology research. Also, PhD thesis research work tends to be highly individual. This is good for his research training, but his exposure to Market and Implementation will be very short and usually comes only indirectly through his advisor via active inclusion and mentorship. During this nominally five year process, significant redirections tend to be difficult upon approaching graduation. While exposure to the iteration process between Technology, Market and Implementation is limited due to the long cycle time of early innovation iterations, his opportunity for individually struggling with uncertainty and excelling at finding new approaches for unsolved Technology problems is maximized.

Innovation Projects offer a very different way of experiencing the iterative process. In the system we've set up at the Innovation Interface, students participate in their own free time in teams composed of experienced innovators and fellow students selected from various complementary disciplines and for their innovation talent. Team members are advised by professors in their fields of expertise, and by members of a corporation with Technology, Market and Implementation knowledge from their side. The experienced innovators are responsible for Innovation Project quality and results for the corporate partner, as well as the professional management of collaborations. The student is free to participate to the best of his ability, while being assured that the team will stay on track and that his back is covered. The degree of innovation training directly correlates with the depth of a student's participation. Students experience no artificial limits to their level of possible engagement other than that they must always give academic tasks priority.

Students receive thorough mentorship corresponding to the level of their engagement, and can increase their weight in the team's decision making as they develop skills throughout the innovation process. However, the projects here are much, much more demanding than typical "class projects" in innovation. They involve innovations-in-progress that are receiving significant corporate resources and can have significant impact on a line of business. The necessity to deliver world-class results on a stringent timeline means that the innovation process sets the pace rather than the student. Different aspects of Technology, Market and Implementation tend to be worked on in parallel and expert depth will be filled in quickly, sometimes overtaking the student temporarily. With the appropriate engagement in a nominally one-year-long Innovation Project, students have the chance to "grow into" the iterative innovation process. Ideally they go through the following stages: (1) somewhat perplexed by what lies ahead and the steep learning curve (never having performed team work on that level and with experts before), (2) an eye-opening realization of what can be accomplished, (3) realizing the importance of deciding what, why, when and how to learn with team coordination, (4) picking up pace and refining skills in targeted learning, abstraction and coordinated decision making, and (5) gaining confidence in performing iterative innovation in other areas.

Innovation training through Fundamental Innovation Research and through an Innovation Project differs naturally in that the former has more day-to-day emphasis on research and the latter has more day-to-day emphasis on innovation iteration. Fundamental Innovation Research provides more opportunity for the student to make his own breakthroughs while an Innovation Project allows the student to become part of the simultaneous breadth and depth of full iterative innovation in a team setting. We believe these two forms are complementary from the innovation education point of view, and may together provide enough training on the university side so that a graduating student can have enough confidence and nascent skills to embark on the path of The Individual Innovator and to continue innovation training self-sufficiently while pursuing his own innovative ideas. Hopefully, students will also participate in mentoring other innovation talent in the future, so that the multiplication effect will help populate every stage of the new innovation pipeline more quickly.

The Role of Government

The pivotal role of government in building a new innovation system, and maintaining it into the future, is that of acting as the investor in fundamental innovation research on behalf of society. This role cannot be fulfilled profitably by any other entity in a competitive market, but it can be enormously profitable for society if fulfilled efficiently. We have seen how the lack of iterative innovation in today's university-government loop caused research to meander towards an increased production of random scientific research. Before we address the government's investor role in more detail, we want to briefly touch upon its roles in the maintenance of a supportive innovation environment and the training of innovators.

We started our discussion on the free-market side by demonstrating that iterative innovation can only be completed efficiently when embedded in free market dynamics. We also pointed out in our analysis of innovation investment that the return on investment for the government's research funding is realized through private returns to various free market participants, and indeed that is the only way it can be realized. Moreover, the lower the barriers for innovation-based transactions are, the better the return for society. We recall these relations from our earlier discussion to underline how critical it is for innovation efficiency to uphold free market dynamics, which ultimately government is responsible for. Many laws uphold and support our free market dynamics, improve the mobility of innovators and partial innovations and keep transactional barriers low, such as patent law, corporate law, employment law and immigration law. Maintaining and optimizing the legal basis for our innovation environment throughout the entire length of the pipeline is a very important role for the government as it also affects the return on investment for society.

When we discussed the training of innovators in the university education context and the self-responsible training after graduation, we assumed that we had a large enough pre-trained and interested pool of talent to draw upon. We know we don't have enough innovators, but do we have enough engineers and scientists? We have not concentrated on the number of engineers and scientists because we do not believe it is a limiting factor at this moment. We are confronted with astonishing numbers of engineers and scientists graduating from Chinese universities, for example, and there is a concern that the U.S. is not keeping pace. However, mean salaries of scientists and engineers in the U.S. have barely doubled in the last 25 years. Considering cost of living increases over a similar time period, it is quite possible that the effective salaries of scientists and engineers have increased very little, if at all. If our economic growth was limited by the supply of engineers and scientists rather than innovators, then the mean salaries would be skyrocketing. Thus, it appears that our first task is to train more innovators among our current scientists and engineers by exposing them to Technology-Market-Implementation experience. This wave of innovators will create rapid growth, possibly creating an economy that would be limited by the supply of engineers and scientists in the future.

How do we expose our currently under-utilized pool of potential innovators in a world in which no organization is optimized for carrying out fundamental innovation over the 10-to-15 year cycle? We must encourage engineers and scientists to move between organizations, acquiring more and more knowledge about Technology-Market-Implementation. Some examples would be to have university researchers spend a significant amount of time periodically in corporations, and also to have company personnel, preferably with engineering and science backgrounds, spend time at a university. Each would participate in innovation projects, and the projects of the potential innovators must be chosen to require all components of Technology-Market-Implementation to maximize learning cycles. Governments can structure programs to incentivize participation of university and company personnel, and organizations like the Innovation Interface can aid in overcoming some of the current barriers in place to such collaboration. Resources applied to this type of activity will be far more effective at stimulating the growth of a new innovation pipeline than blindly increasing research funding using the current model.

Now let's return to the innovation-investor role of government. In an effort to help move their nations' economies quickly up the economic ladder, universities in fast-growing countries have ramped up basic research activities that are largely funded by their governments. This path is logical, as it is hard to imagine having a high-tech economy without scientists and engineers. The blind funding of basic science without an emphasis on innovation has nonetheless been done at such a pace that many countries are approaching catch-up with the U.S. system, so much so that they appear to be overshooting the optimum innovation state. Recall that the U.S. system organically grew the time horizon of research investment in the first half of the twentieth century, resulting in a sea of practical engineers and scientists connecting concepts across vocational fields with basic science. Since rising countries have largely followed the U.S.-style system of today, as opposed to the state of the system in 1950, the result is a vast global library of random science which can be accessed by anyone using the Internet. Although it is important to keep filling this reservoir, the value of an additional random piece of research in this global oversupply of "random scientific research" knowledge is close to zero. However, the value of a piece of fundamental innovation research, grounded in the iterative innovation process and thus purposefully connected to other Technology as well as Market and Implementation, is large.

It is extraordinarily difficult for a nation-state to try and bias research investment towards fundamental innovation research and away from the random kind. After all, performing random scientific research is generally much easier. The current system makes research investment decisions based predominately on paper proposals. Paper proposals do not reveal the proposer's intent effectively. For example, two identical proposals can speak to the intent of impacting particular applications and imply a desire for innovation, but the authors of the two proposals could have very different real intent. This difficulty is not surprising, as private financial investors do not rely only on paper business plans. In fact, due diligence into the individuals and meetings to try and determine their intent and character are critical to maximizing the investors' return. We are forced to conclude that the current funding mechanisms are incapable of shifting research investments towards fundamental innovation research.

What can we learn from past research investing? Although much of the actual fundamental innovation research took place in the corporate laboratories of the past, we know that government investments in university research were also much more innovation-relevant during that time. In the chapter on The American Innovation System we discussed how the better alignment was due to government closely observing the signals that came from and passed between the corporate labs, in order to identify what research investments were needed. If we take the organizational component out of the equation, we can see that what government research investors were really doing was tracking the various iterative innovation processes. Since they did not have full transparency of the innovation processes taking place within the walls of the corporate laboratories, the government investors *had* to observe "signals". This was a reliable process because they knew that the sources of these signals could be trusted. It is important to note, too, that the corporate labs did not really play an active role in the government-university funding loop — they primarily made the information from the iterative innovation processes available. To use a chemistry analogy, information from the iterative innovation processes was the catalyst in the overall government-university reaction. Projecting these insights onto today's environment, two points seem obvious. First, changing some incentives, like requesting more innovation metrics from researchers that really have no access to them, or changing some administrative mechanisms is unlikely to change the dynamics between the two huge bureaucracies of government and universities in a significant way. In terms of our chemical analogy, this would be like changing the temperature slightly and expecting the nature of the reaction to change. Second, it is possible that new organizations, like the Innovation Interface, would be capable of acting as a catalyst by providing the information from innovation process iterations to help focus research investments towards fundamental innovation research.

Making the iterative innovation process part of research investment considerations can enable valuable savings if fast-failure mechanisms were to be invoked when the innovation processes are shown not to converge — recall our example of Buckyballs and carbon nanotubes. It can also reveal valuable information upfront when the iterative innovation process cannot be applied very well. The biotech-pharma sector is an interesting such case. As the economics of small molecule drug discovery in major pharmaceutical firms started to become inefficient, early biotech-pharma companies such as Genentech in 1975 painted a vision of an increased rate of drug discovery and drug efficiency, offering a potential "new innovation path" through the use of new technologies.

Interestingly, multitudes of biotech-pharma companies also found it possible to perform IPOs, most of them without operating profit. After 30 years, Gary Pisano's 2006 book *Science Business: the Promise, the Reality and the Future of Biotech* showed that biotech-pharma had not increased drug discovery or efficiency. This is not surprising when we look at the pharmaceutical sector from the iterative innovation process point of view. First of all, the target Market is largely fixed: one drug development for one health condition (disregarding off-label uses, reformulations etc.).

Second, there is little uncertainty in Implementation because the business model is largely fixed by the industry practices of health insurers paying the reimbursements for the drugs, the medical practitioners writing the prescriptions, the clinical trail system in place for ensuring the safety and efficacy of new products, and very little room for flexibility in manufacturing, intellectual property protection and other matters. So there is not really any significant feedback that could influence the path of Technology by iterative innovation across the elements. On the Technology side, we did not build the human body and still know very little about it, so our safety and efficacy predictors are poor. Without having to get into any more specifics, it is already clear that drug development has been and still is "discovery science research" governed largely by trial and error rather than "fundamental innovation research" governed by the iterative innovation process. In one sense, this sector is close to true linear innovation (i.e. the funnel picture), and its inefficiency is indicative of the inefficiencies of linear innovation. The false biotech-pharma "innovation" narrative simply pushed the cost of drug discovery research back down the pipeline — from big pharma to both the shareholders of biotech IPO companies and the government through its university research funding during hype waves.

Government investment in fundamental innovation research has been most successful historically, and is still so today, when the government is also a customer. In this case, the government provides Market and Implementation context, but it is also a driving force behind the iterative innovation process because it wants real results. Additional success for government acting as a customer-investor arises from its ability to continue the support further into the innovation gap. We have discussed the importance of Small Business Innovative Research (SBIR) funding and customer-investor government funding for crossing the "valley of death", and we've given the historical example of the role that the Department of Defense (DoD) played as a customer-investor in the birth of the semiconductor industry.

The government can increase its research investment efficiency in areas where commercial markets and government markets overlap by invoking the more effective customer-investor research investment model. But possible Market distortions should be assessed critically upfront, because they can cause innovations to converge differently or make them dependent on continued government demand, which may or may not be tolerable depending on intent. If an area is identified in which innovation can be truly dual-use, then the government can invest without distorting the innovation outcome and take full advantage of the customer-investor efficiency and maybe also increase the SBIR funding available. The historical example of DoD's role in the birth of the semiconductor industry was a case of such true dual use. Iterative innovation was not distorted because the Market and Technology needs of government electronic systems were the same as the needs for commercial systems: high speed, lower power consumption, high power efficiency. However, in systems where cost was not a constraint, there was no guarantee that there would be dual use. But in this case, the government was a real customer needing the functionality of these components regardless of dual-use benefits. Fortunately, even in this case, some synergy could be found in commercial markets. Note that the semiconductor and integrated circuit technology investments are highly unusual, and that the majority of government needs are not as synergistic with the marketplace. If innovations from government customer-investor activities have no overlap at all with the commercial marketplace, then no net economic growth will be created. But the precise extent of potential dual use is of course not known upfront.

To illustrate the kind of upfront thinking warranted when the extent of dual use is unclear and Market distortions are likely, let's consider an example in the energy sector. We would like to emphasize that this discussion is intended only to provide some additional clarity about the customer-investor option. The dynamics we're trying to illustrate may apply in other sectors as well as energy. As the total energy consumed by government infrastructure is sizable, sufficient market overlap can in principle exist to make the customer-investor model work. However, Market distortions may be difficult to avoid. As an example, solar technology has been supported in other countries for three to four decades with government programs, primarily by Germany and Japan subsidizing their homeowners' markets, which in turn subsidized solar technology companies. Germany has also provided incentives for homeowners to improve the energy efficiencies of their houses for a long time, which benefited various industries separately, such as construction and appliances. The only way to bring together all the factors that affect the total energy budget of a building is via its owner, which is what many of these subsidy programs do. But it is only possible to nudge incremental innovations of the various components of the total "building energy system" in this fashion, as the components are spread over various industries and the individual homeowner has no power with respect to novel system integration.

But what could solutions look like if one were to remove all these constraints, and call forth fundamental innovation, through a building owner able to take advantage of new material properties, consider different air flow management systems, eliminate some AC-DC electricity conversions by solar panel integration, introduce new control systems and so forth, whether for retrofit or new buildings? Owning many buildings, the government could be the customer of such potentially more fundamental innovations while investing in the research necessary to generate them. The government may have an additional strategic intent, for example that of energy self-sufficiency for security purposes, which may make the government as a customer willing to pay more than a private entity. Whether or not there would be enough overlap for solutions to be competitive in the commercial marketplace ten years later, one cannot know upfront. But that is for the iterative innovation process to decide. The whole "building energy system" has plenty of uncertainty in Technology, Market and Implementation for medium-term or fundamental innovation. With the government as a customer and if the innovation iterations converge to meet its overall needs, the innovation can be finished in the marketplace, iterating through the complex supply chains across several industries, even including proper system commissioning. Maybe only some parts will find dual use, maybe none will and the innovation is only good for the security need of the government. Maybe the innovation iterations will not converge, so they should be abandoned.

The point of this example is not about energy or buildings, but about the fact that the route of subsidizing the homeowner directly incentivizes primarily incremental innovations and can result in significant Market distortions, whereas "fundamental research investments" via the customer-investor model can create options that may be more effective and less distorting, if the overlap of markets could allow it.

We need to point out that the individual innovator or entrepreneur is focused on a much more micro-economical goal in that he is concerned predominately with his company's or his innovation's success, and not net growth of the nation-state. Thus, the innovator or entrepreneur can still benefit from the iterative innovation process even if the Market and Implementation are distorted by governments. For example, entrepreneurs with successful solar technology companies have seen an annual growth rate of 30% while subsidies were in place. Thus, an innovator or entrepreneur and his investors can gain enormously by executing in an environment where government subsidies exist. However, governments should realize that such stimulated industries do not produce net growth unless successful innovation iteration factors impact non-subsidized markets. For security reasons a nation-state may, for example, incentivize solar energy innovation, but only the resulting Market distortions allow the innovations to be sustained. In such a process, the government is redistributing tax revenues from the citizens to solar innovators. This process is very different from the process in the semiconductor-PC-IT paradigm, where non-governmental consumers of integrated circuits, personal computers, and software directly rewarded the innovators, and the innovations produced true overall economic growth.

As our nation struggles with the need to restructure many of its programs, we realize that the core nation-state funding of "random scientific research" is insufficient to heal the innovation pipeline. Likewise, our entire model of stimulating innovation also needs restructuring. Following the implications of iterative innovation, any innovation or research investment in any organizations, new and old, should be aligned with the critical need for having *individuals* acquire all elements of Technology-Market-Implementation to support the long-term goal of maintaining our innovation society.

We say this because, ultimately, it is not any systems or policies that innovate. It's people like you.